THE INTENTIONALITY MODEL AND LANGUAGE ACQUISITION: ENGAGEMENT, EFFORT, AND THE ESSENTIAL TENSION IN DEVELOPMENT

Lois Bloom
Erin Tinker

WITH COMMENTARY BY
Ellin Kofsky Scholnick

Willis F. Overton
Series Editor

MONOGRAPHS OF THE SOCIETY FOR RESEARCH IN CHILD DEVELOPMENT
Serial No. 267, Vol. 66, No. 4, 2001

1-02

48677681

BLACKWELL
Publishers

Boston, Massachusetts   Oxford, United Kingdom

THE INTENTIONALITY MODEL AND LANGUAGE ACQUISITION: ENGAGEMENT, EFFORT, AND THE ESSENTIAL TENSION IN DEVELOPMENT

CONTENTS

COMMENTARY

ABSTRACT

BLOOM, LOIS, and TINKER, ERIN. The Intentionality Model and Language Acquisition: Engagement, Effort, and the Essential Tension in Development. *Monographs of the Society for Research in Child Development*, 2001, **66**(4, Serial No. 267).

The purpose of the longitudinal research reported in this *Monograph* was to examine language acquisition in the second year of life in the context of developments in cognition, affect, and social connectedness. The theoretical focus for the research is on the agency of the child and the importance of the child's intentionality for explaining development, rather than on language as an independent object. The model of development for the research is a Model of Intentionality with two components: the engagement in a world of persons and objects that motivates acquiring a language, and the effort that is required to express and articulate increasingly discrepant and elaborate intentional state representations. The fundamental assumption in the model is that the driving force for acquiring language is in the essential tension between engagement and effort for linguistic, emotional, and physical actions of interpretation and expression. Results of lag sequential analyses are reported to show how different behaviors—words, sentences, emotional expressions, conversational interactions, and constructing thematic relations between objects in play—converged, both in the stream of children's actions in everyday events, in real time, and in developmental time between the emergence of words at about 13 months and the transition to simple sentences at about 2 years of age. Patterns of deviation from baseline rates of the different behaviors show that child emotional expression, child speech, and mother speech clearly influence each other, and the mutual influences between them are different at times of either emergence or achievement in both language and object play. The three conclusions that follow from the results of the research are that (a) expression and interpretation are the acts of performance in which language is learned, which means that performance counts for explaining language acquisition; (b) language is not an independent object but is acquired by a child in relation to other kinds of behaviors and their development; and (c) acquiring language in coordination with other behaviors in acts of expression and interpretation takes work, so that acquiring language is not easy.

I. INTRODUCTION

Three themes prevail in the theoretical rationale and research reported in this *Monograph*. The first is the *integration* of language with other developments in what are ordinarily called different developmental domains. The second is the origin of development in general and language acquisition in particular in the *intentionality* and action of the infant and young child. The third theme is the *essential tension* between engagement and effort that drives human development and, by inclusion, the acquisition of language, forward.

AN INTEGRATIVE PERSPECTIVE

Both the external behaviors that we see and hear and the hidden representations in intentional states that give rise to them exist only in relation to other aspects of human functioning. Each aspect of development touches on all its other aspects. The articulation of this fundamental principle of development is usually attributed to Heinz Werner: for example, "every behavioral act, whether outward bodily movement or internalized cognitive operation, gains its significance and status in terms of its role in the overall functioning of the organism" (Werner & Kaplan, 1963, pp. 4–5).

Werner's developmental principle has always been at least implicit in research and theory in developmental psychology, but it is seldom made explicit, much less studied directly. For example, although "real infants live and develop in a world filled with people, things, and events in continuous interaction" (Thelen & Smith, 1994, p. xii), such interactions have not as yet been the focus of study within the dynamic systems perspective. Human functioning and development have long been conceptualized in terms of systems theory and dynamical systems, but the theory rarely finds its way into research practices. Instead, the trend in developmental research has been "towards ever increasing fragmentation of the object of study" (Overton, 2002, p. 39). Motor, cognitive, affective, and social developments tend to be studied only in controlled laboratory situations and independently of one another (Bloom, 1998).

The separation of categories of behavior for purposes of both research and theory has a long history in "a methodological tradition . . . [that] depends on the separation of natural processes into isolable parts for individual study. It has provided a rich repertoire of information about the world, but it systematically ignores the aspects of reality that involve relations between the separated processes" (Bidell, 1988, p. 330). What is lost is "the person as a vital integrated embodied center of agency and action," a person for whom categories of behavior are not separated but fundamentally and coherently integrated (Overton, 2002, p. 39).

This tradition in developmental psychology and research has been licensed most recently by the modularity view of human cognition. In modular theories, learning occurs in different domains and "benefits from multiple mental structures that support attention to and learning about domain relevant" data rather than from general, homogeneous processes (Gelman & Williams, 1998, p. 584). Arguably, modularity theories have come about in large part because what we study tends to determine its explanation. When language has been the object of study, specifically linguistic theories have been invoked to explain not only the phenomena of language itself but how it is acquired as well.

Modularity theory and research in language acquisition have become increasingly mechanistic and deterministic, invoking mechanisms that are only and specifically linguistic and outside of the child's control. Such mechanisms include actual and hypothesized brain mechanisms; computational systems; and lexical principles, constraints, or biases for word learning. For example, in advancing what arguably became the most influential theory in linguistics, Chomsky (1965) introduced the "language acquisition device," an embodied linguistic mechanism in the brain that controls language and its acquisition. His theory of biologically specified linguistic representations that direct the acquisition of language has since been given an even more explicit determinism in the form of an "instinct" or "gene" for language (Pinker, 1994).

In connectionist models, language acquisition is reduced to the neurological architecture of the brain and the neural connections that are the effects of linguistic experience (e.g., Klahr & MacWhinney, 1998; Rumelhart & McClelland, 1986). However, whatever covert corollary activity occurs in the brain, language is fundamentally psychological and depends on mental representations. The representations expressed by language cannot be reduced to physiological form or function because these have neither mental content nor meaning (Searle, 1992), and without mental content, physiology by itself has no efficacy for explaining language acquisition.

2

Neither development in general nor language acquisition in particular can be reduced to material neural networks (Bloom, 1993a; Overton, 2002).

Yet another influential model of word learning promotes attention and perceptual analyses for associative learning as preeminently deterministic and causal (Smith, 2000). Few would argue against the view that associative learning has to figure in almost any theory of language acquisition, but association is just one component of the word learning process among many. Moreover, associations of the sort needed for language acquisition have, themselves, to be mentally represented in consciousness before they can be recorded as knowledge representations. Finally, attentional and perceptual processes depend on dynamic mental activity by the child and are far from the automatic, much less the "dumb," mechanisms that Smith (p. 54) describes.

Perhaps the most influential contemporary theories to explain word learning in particular invoke constraints, principles, or biases that are, in effect, prescriptions for specific aspects of the word learning process. One example is the *whole object principle*, in which novel words name whole objects rather than object parts or properties (Markman, 1989). Another example is the *novel name-nameless category principle*, where a novel word names an object that does not yet have a name (Golinkoff, Hirsh-Pasek, Bailey, & Wenger, 1992). The defining characteristic of all such constraints on learning is that they are linguistically specific—that is, they apply only for learning language—and, even more specifically, they apply only to learning words. However, in response to criticisms of lexical principles from a more child-centric perspective (e.g., Bloom, 1993a, 1998; Bloom, Tinker, & Margulis, 1993; Nelson, 1988), lexical principles are now contextualized in the social-pragmatic context (e.g., Hollich, Hirsh-Pasek, & Golinkoff, 2000; Woodward & Markman, 1998) and attention to perceptual cues (Hollich et al., 2000).

Young children's cognitive development does not seem to have been taken seriously, as yet, in conjunction with lexical principles (Bloom, 2000c), in particular development of *concepts* and conceptual structure for an understanding of the world and the *symbolic capacity* for making possible the representations in mind that refer to what a child understands of the world. The key question that remains then is: What do lexical principles contribute to word learning over and above the perceptual, cognitive, social, and other developments that are required? Lexical principles seem to lose considerable *explanatory* force the more they require contextualization in the rest of the child's behavior and development for their operation, however much they may succeed in *describing* aspects of the word learning process.

The result of deterministic, specifically linguistic, theories and research based on them is that both the child and the child's behaviors have come to be treated as "objects." Language as an object is ordinarily conceptualized at several hierarchical levels of analysis, from Language writ large in its most abstract epistemic sense, at the top, to the linguistic units of sentence procedures, words, and sounds that the language subsumes, at the bottom. Words and sentences thereby assume a life of their own, apart from the child who produced them and apart from the situations in which the child said them (or signed them). With advances in technology, words and sentences appear on computer monitors or on checklist reports, and the children are missing. The child, then, is also an object, the absent learner of the linguistic units. Causality is attributed either to language itself—that is, the child learns the linguistic units because the child is learning the language—or to the computational or neurological mechanisms that serve language in the brain.

We do, certainly, need to look at one or another aspect of language, isolate it, and manipulate it in order to study it. But we need to consider what it means when we take the units of language out of the very fabric of the child's life in which they are necessarily embedded. When the units and procedures of the language are separated from the so-called extraneous variables of performance, then the language the child is learning becomes disembodied and decontextualized (Bloom, 2000c).

When causality in language acquisition is assigned to factors that are external to the child's agency and intentionality, such as maturation, innate knowledge, or genetics, then we stop looking for processes of developmental change. The result is description only of what *is*, what children can and cannot do, and correlations between behaviors and chronological age, or between behaviors and anatomy. Age, however, is only an index, it is not a causal variable. Age only reduces to time, and time causes nothing (e.g., Overton, 1998; Wohlwill, 1970). Anatomy, likewise, is the product of maturation and only reduces to biological and neurological tissue that cannot cause actions, such as actions of expression and interpretation essential to learning and development. *Actions are caused by the people who plan, execute, evaluate, and control them.* Changes in linguistic behaviors may be correlated with time but are not caused by it; changes in language may be enabled by the brain but are not caused by it. We still need to identify the variables and processes of change for language acquisition, and these might or might not be correlated with age and anatomy, and often have to do with factors ordinarily considered to lie outside of language.

The child also becomes an object when explanatory mechanisms are attributed to other persons in the social context who provide linguistic input along with a supporting environment for learning from it. The child is the receiver of the input and supports for learning, as in traditional scaffolding theory (e.g., Ninio & Bruner, 1978), or the beneficiary of the

4

pragmatic, social signals that others provide for cues to understanding, as in more recent social-pragmatic theories (e.g., Baldwin, 1993; Tomasello & Akhtar, 1995). The language, then, becomes the secondary object as the medium of the transactions. Causality is attributed to the transactions themselves or to the social, functional goals they serve. That is, the child learns language because the child receives social and pragmatic cues along with the linguistic units, and the transactions between child and other "work" to get things done in the world.

However, children's actions of expression and interpretation are explanatory for language acquisition: "All the functions of language—including its instrumental, interpersonal, and problem-solving functions—absolutely depend on the power of language for expression and interpretation. . . . Language can succeed in influencing other persons in social contexts [and getting things done in the world] only to the extent that language connects the contents of individual minds" (Bloom, 1993a, pp. 13–14; see also Overton, 1998, for discussion of the expressive-constitutive and instrumental-communicative functions of action). Somehow, the child has to be kept in the picture as the major player, as the *agent* of the practices that contribute to the acquisition process, practices that have "primacy in the emergence of selfhood" and are "pivotal to our knowledge of the world." The multiple sources of the self are to be found in the natural, practical, and social aspects of life, "allowing the social its part in our constitution, without making all that we are the gift of society" (Archer, 2000, p. 318).

In sum, in most theories of language acquisition, the child is often an object and essentially a passive receiver of physical or social cues, or the locus of brain mechanisms or hypothetical constraints, biases, or heuristic principles that filter the available information for the child. Missing in such theoretical accounts of the acquisition process is the *authority of the child*. What a child has in mind—the child's intentional state at any particular moment of time—is expressed by the child's actions and interactions and interpreted from others' expressions, and it is these acts of expression and interpretation that determine development.

Admitting the agency of the child into the language acquisition process has two consequences. First, considering the child as subject rather than object forces us to see language as one part of development more generally, and to look at language more closely in relation to other aspects of development, as has begun to happen now in several different research paradigms (e.g., Hoff & Naigles, 2002; Hollich et al., 2000; Imai & Haryu, 2001). One purpose of the research reported in this *Monograph* is to show that behaviors and developments in different domains are not independent of each other. Language depends on and emerges out of a nexus of closely connected developments in cognition, emotion, and social interaction in the first three years of life. Language is not acquired apart from a child's cognitive, emotional, and social development, any more than developments in other aspects of cognition or in emotion or social interaction happen apart from each other or independently of language (e.g., Bloom, 1970, 1973, 1993a, 1998). Accordingly, in the research reported here, we set out to determine how different behaviors (words, sentences, emotional expressions, actions in play, and conversations) converge, both from moment to moment in the stream of children's actions and interactions in real time, and in developmental time extending over the second year of life.

The second consequence of including the agency of the child in the process of language acquisition is to invoke *the child's intentionality* for explaining development. The central role of intentionality for acquiring language and the basic tenets of the Intentionality Model were first described by Bloom, Beckwith, Capatides, and Hafitz (1988), who underscored the importance of *unobservable representations in the mind* that are expressed first by emotion, before language, and then also expressed by language as it emerges in the second year of life. Because a child's expressions and interpretations are *about* these intentional state representations, they are fundamental phenomena for language and its acquisition. Intentional states are dynamically constructed from moment to moment in that dimension of mind ordinarily referred to as consciousness, as prior knowledge informs perceptions, actions, and interactions in the world. Intentionality, in the larger sense, is that aspect of mind that intervenes between perceptions and knowledge—that is, between perception and apprehension of the world at any one moment in time, and knowledge of the world from experience as it exists in memory all of the time (see also Campbell, 1979, 1986).

Intentional states include representation of elements, roles, and relations that are about objects, events, and relations in the world. They are constructed under psychological attitudes of belief, desire, and feeling toward them and are expressed by the actions, words, and emotional displays of everyday behaviors. Although unobservable and hidden, they are not mysterious, because the child constructs them and owns them. And they are not mysterious to other persons either, because the child acts to express them.

In sum, the goal of the intentionality model and the research reported in this *Monograph* is to underscore the importance for language learning of the dynamic contents of mind that are expressed by the child's actions and interpreted from the actions of other persons. The emphasis in the model is on the child's cognition and action for explaining language acquisition, rather than on the physiology of the brain, the language itself as an object, or other mechanisms as explanation that operate outside of (i.e., do not admit) mental content and process in states of consciousness.

THE INTENTIONALITY MODEL

Intentionality theories of human behavior have a long history in philosophy, beginning with Aristotle and continuing through Descartes to Brentano (1966), to Husserl at the turn of the last century (e.g., the papers in Dreyfus, 1982), and to such contemporary theorists as Bratman (1987), Danto (1973), Dennett (1978), Fauconnier (1985), Searle (1983, 1992), and Taylor (1985). An intentionality perspective has been relatively rare in psychology (e.g., Bruner, 1981; Campbell, 1979, 1986) but has been developed most recently in research and theory in the acquisition of theory of mind and social understanding (e.g., Malle, Moses, & Baldwin, 2001; Zelazo, Astington, & Olson, 1999).

A primary assumption in this *Monograph* is that development in general and acquiring a language in particular are grounded in the child's intentionality, which means that understanding language and the explanation of language acquisition have to take consciousness very seriously (see Searle, 1992). A child's intentionality has an impact on development in at least two ways. First, the mental contents of consciousness can be expressed by actions, including the sensorimotor actions of infancy, emotional displays, speech, and play. In turn, the effect of expression and its counterpart, interpretation, is to revise and change the contents of intentional states with representation of new elements, roles, and relations. Therefore, the consequence of acting in general and expression and interpretation in particular is the construction of new representations in consciousness that contribute to what the child knows about the world. Second, because expressions of intentional states embody a child's beliefs, desires, and feelings and make them manifest, contents of mind can be shared with others who interpret and respond to them. Intersubjectivity between child and other, therefore, depends upon acts of expression and interpretation, and the child's participation in a social world is promoted by the expression and mutual interpretation of intentional states (Bloom, 1993a; papers in Zelazo et al., 1999).

Intentionality and Embodiment

In the program of research begun by Bloom and colleagues (Bloom & Capatides, 1987b; Bloom, Beckwith, Capatides, & Hafitz, 1988; Bloom & Beckwith, 1989) and continued in this *Monograph*, we chose to study children's words, emotional expressions, play with objects, and conversational interactions with their mothers as the external, observable, public embodiments of the internal, hidden, personal, private intentional states they made manifest. An expression is "a set of material properties . . . [that] embody a given representation" (Danto, 1983, p. 252). An expression "makes something manifest in an embodiment" and a criterial feature of expressions is that "their expressing/saying/manifesting is something that they do . . . rather than something that can happen through them" (Taylor, 1979, pp. 73, 76). Thus, the meaning of different expressions (a word, a smile, a gesture or other action) originates in our intentionality, and how such different expressions converge in the stream of everyday activities depends on the dynamic practices that embody intentional states.

In contrast to this intentionality position, human behavior and development are often explained in terms of physiological and neurological embodiments apart from psychological meaning. An example is in the concept of "the embodied mind" for explaining "mind-body-world interconnections" and how human cognition "arises from bodily interactions with the world and is continually enmeshed with them" (Thelen, 2000, pp. 3–5). Although nominally dedicated to understanding human behavior in its many and varied forms, this concept of embodiment embraces only the neurology of the brain and the physiology of bodily action for explanation. For example, after describing the elegant details and patterns of infant kicking to activate a mobile, Thelen asks "What does this *mean* for the baby?" (emphasis added). Her answer invokes the "strength and nature of the perceptual-motor pathways that access higher functions" (pp. 15–17), as embodied in the dense system of neuronal interconnections in the brain. The diagrams given of such interconnections do not include connections to the *psychological content* of what the movements are about or why the baby kicks. According to Thelen, "the ultimate job of the central nervous system is to move the body, including the muscles of speech"[!], but surely movements of the body are not without representational, motivational, and affective psychological content.

There are, then, these two notions (at least) of embodiment: the cognition for physical movement such as kicking and reaching embodied in physiology and brain activity (Thelen, 2000), on the one hand, and, on the other hand, intentional state representations embodied by the material properties of expressive actions such as speech, emotion, and play with objects (Bloom, 1993a), and other embodied "practices" of everyday life (Archer, 2000). These different embodiments reflect the frequent confound between levels of description and levels of explanation, between *ontology*, what one chooses to study; *epistemology*, how we find out about it; and *causation*, what something does or how it works, as described by Searle (1992, p. 18). Explanation typically follows description, so that what one chooses to study not only dictates the instrument of analysis but also becomes the source of explanation. Thelen and colleagues chose to study the motor activities of infant kicking and reaching, and they explain kicking and reaching in terms of their physiological and neurological embodiments.

In the research studies reported in this *Monograph*, we looked at the intricate patterning and coordination of different expressive actions as they unfolded in relation to each other in real time in the practices of ordinary activity. We have no doubt that the patterns and interrelations we describe here have a physiologically based component for the motor movements that produced them, and a neurologically based component for the interconnections in the brain that serve them, and hence a physical, anatomical embodiment. However, our concern is with expressive actions as embodiments of psychological representations, and the attribution of mental phenomena that such actions license for explaining developmental processes in general and language acquisition in particular. More generally, "embodiment creates a seamless bridge between the biological, the psychological, and the sociocultural . . . referring both to the body as physical structure, and the body as a form of lived experience, actively engaged in the world" (Overton, 2002, p. 39).

The Intentionality Model and Psychological Process

Intentionality can include the goal-directed ordinary sense of intention to do something that is "just one form of Intentionality along with belief, hope, fear, desire, and lots of others" (Searle, 1983, p. 3). When an infant reaches for a toy, for example, the reaching is intended by the infant and goal-directed, but this intention to act in the ordinary sense is just one part of what the infant has in mind. The "infant's intentional state also includes, along with a representation of the toy and the desire to have it, representations of feelings about having or not having it, beliefs about what the object is and what might be done with it, awareness of whether another person might help to achieve it, perhaps a plan for doing something with it once it is achieved, and so on" (Bloom, 2000b, p. 179). Aspects of these intentional contents can be expressed affectively, linguistically, or by acting in other ways.

The process whereby intentional states are constructed out of the data from perception and prior knowledge is schematized in Figure 1. The labeled components in the process and the arrows connecting them represent the flow of dynamic mental activity that sets up representations for interpretation, expression, and new knowledge. Prior Knowledge includes knowledge of other persons, objects, relationships, and events. Perception, informed by this prior knowledge, includes both linguistic and social input

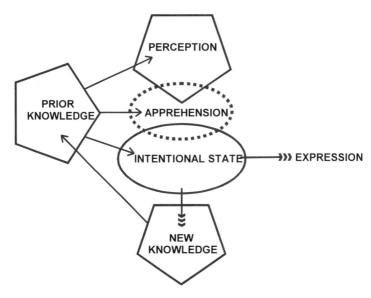

FIGURE 1.—Origins and processes in constructing intentional states.

along with data from the physical world. Data from perception and prior knowledge are briefly apprehended relative to present Intentional State representations, which thereby change to accommodate them. The processes captured by these components, their connections, and the dynamic flow between them are mental processes, they are in the child's mind— part of the *psychology* rather than the biology or neurology of the child.

The dynamic components and processes in the Intentionality Model are a laterally patterned "narrative" or "relational" account of the "stratification of psychological life"; they do not constitute a hierarchy of levels of causes and their effects in a causal "essentialist or entity-based" account (Chandler and Sokol, 2002, pp. 4–6; Overton, 1998). Components and process run off together: Perception and apprehension are continuous, not discrete, as they inform changing, dynamically constructed intentional state representations. Causality in the Intentionality Model is in the agency of the child. It is the child who perceives, who apprehends, who constructs the intentional state, who acts to express it, and who interprets what others do (including what they say) to construct a new intentional state. These are not unconscious, automatic processes that run according to a prescribed schedule of contingencies. They could not be automatic, given that virtually all events (even those for which the child might have learned a "script") have unexpected and unpredictable aspects.

10

The child as the agent of expressive and interpretive acts is Piaget's child. In Piaget's theory (e.g., 1952, 1954), children learn about the world through their actions, actions that are sensorimotor in infancy before they are transformed into increasingly abstract and complex forms of thought. In early infancy, contents of mind are constrained to the data of perception and actions—what the infant has in mind is about what the infant is seeing and doing in the moment, and hence sensorimotor. A good example is the very young infant who has a representation in mind of the mobile visible above the crib, along with the memory trace of it moving, and acts by kicking to reactivate the mobile again (see the extensive research program described and summarized by Rovee-Collier, 1997).

With developments in the symbolic capacity, knowledge, and procedures for recalling knowledge from memory, infants begin to recall objects and actions from the past and anticipate them in the future. Thus, contents of mind continue to be influenced by, but not constrained to, perception and action (Bloom, Beckwith, Capatides, & Hafitz, 1988; Thelen, 2000). All actions, including sensorimotor actions, originate in representations that we ascribe to the child's intentional state. Just as children learn and develop through their actions on the world (Piaget, 1954; see also Archer, 2000; Sheets-Johnston, 2000), children learn the language through their actions of interpretation and expression (e.g., Bloom, 1991, 1993a).

But the child in the Intentionality Model is very much Piaget's child for yet another reason. The progress Piaget described from sensorimotor to increasingly representational forms of thought is progress in the very processes that result in increasingly discrepant and increasingly elaborated mental states. The developments in thinking that he described were developments that change the nature of the representations in consciousness; sensorimotor, concrete, and formal thought are forms of thought whereby the mental contents of intentionality are constructed. Piaget's ultimate concern was the construction of knowledge, how the young infant and child come to understand reality and know about the world. The child's knowledge structures consist of theories of objects, space, causality, and so forth (e.g., Piaget, 1954, 1967, 1974). These theories are represented at the level of knowledge in long-term memory. However, the processes of thinking and the representation of the contents of reality whereby knowledge and theories develop take place at the level of consciousness. They are the processes and representations of intentionality.

Intentional states include *psychological attitudes* (e.g., belief, desire, feeling) directed toward *propositional content* that is about persons, objects, and events in the world, as schematized in Figure 2. The model, therefore, embraces the *affective* as well as the *cognitive* life of the child without,

11

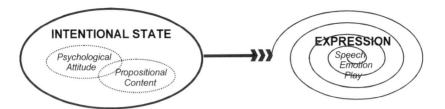

FIGURE 2.—Components of intentional states and kinds of expression.

however, advocating a duality of affect and cognition since the one necessarily informs and supports the other. Forms of expression are varied and can overlap in time (e.g., talking while smiling, or talking or smiling while playing with objects). The focus of the research reported here is on the microgenesis of these different expressions, and how the temporal relations between them change over time as a function of developments in language, cognition, emotion, and social interaction in the second year.

The Intentionality Model is avowedly a psychological model with the child's agency at its center and, as such, might appear to ignore the social world. However, there is no social world apart from the child's perception, apprehension, and intentional stance toward it (see Archer, 2000). For a socially based explanation of behavior to be meaningful, it has to consider the extent to which what persons in the context do and their relationships to the child enter into the representations the child has in mind. *Society and culture have meaning only to the extent that other persons and their activity are represented in mind*—represented in the long-term mental contents of prior knowledge as a consequence of past experience, and in the short-term contents of perception, apprehension, and intentionality in present action. If other persons are not a part of these representations, or cannot be introduced to them, then they stand outside of the child's experience and simply cannot exist for the child. Social and cultural contexts, therefore, are as intrinsic to the Intentionality Model as is the physical context.

Personal and Interpersonal Intentionality

The intentionality model shifts the balance of influence from the adult to the child for the dynamics of their interactions that serve language acquisition (e.g., Bloom, 1993a; Bloom, Margulis, Tinker, & Fujita, 1996). The child's agenda—what the child has in mind—in the interactions creates the language-learning scenario more often than not and

12

sets the pace for language learning. Language learning scenarios are, to be sure, joint products between a child and other persons; in the current idiom, they are co-constructed between child and other, and indeed it could not be otherwise. Language tutor and child have to talk (or sign) to each other and relate to each other in more or less reasonable and productive ways. To describe the language acquisition process as a co-construction is accurate, but co-construction cannot bypass the basic fact that it is the child's interpretation of what another person does or says that changes what the child has in mind. Targets of learning have to be represented in the child's conscious states of mind.

Contents of intentional states, although personal and private in the sense that they are internal and truly known only by the child, can be constructed out of a continuous cycle of reciprocal interpretation. Nevertheless they are not exclusively or necessarily social. To say that "many individual actions are best characterized in collective [or "collaborative"] terms" (Gibbs, 2001, pp. 109–113) does not diminish the necessity or force of the representational process in an individual mind. "Neither the context nor the person's activities can ultimately be defined independently ... meanings derive from their integration in the psychological event" (Rogoff, 1982, p. 132). Similarly, we can speak of linguistic units in another's message "setting up" mental elements, roles, and relations as Fauconnier (1985) describes. But linguistic units can set up mental contents only by virtue of the child who constructs the representation in mind.

When intentionality is invoked in social pragmatic theories it is by and large a second-person perspective in a theory of *the other mind*: how children learn to attribute intentional states to other persons; how they come to understand the intentionality of other persons and the sources of others' intentional actions; or how other persons can influence the child's thoughts and, hence, the child's actions (Baldwin, 1993; Tomasello, 1999; see also several of the papers in Malle et al., 2001 and Zelazo et al., 1999). Missing in social pragmatic theories and in models of lexical principles-plus-pragmatics (e.g., Woodward & Markman, 1998) is a first-person perspective on *the child's contents of mind*. What the child has in mind prompts and exploits the pragmatic cues from a caregiver for word learning, and kindles and fuels the interactions in which such cues occur and the units of language are learned. To be sure, the child is the novice and the adult is the expert in language learning. But that fact cannot obscure the child's agency in acts of interpretation and expression directed toward other persons—acts that embody, make manifest, express what the child has in mind (Bloom, 1993a, 1998, 2000a). The intentionality model exposes and emphasizes the child's part without diminishing either the importance or the effect of the child's partners in their exchanges.

THE ORIGINS OF DEVELOPMENT IN INTENTIONALITY: ENGAGEMENT AND EFFORT

The Intentionality Model has two components, *engagement* and *effort*, that interact with language in the process of its acquisition; and it has three explanatory principles, the principles of *relevance, discrepancy,* and *elaboration.* Following a description of the model, we show how it has been tested so far in previous research. The period from late infancy through the second birthday is distinguished by substantial progress in language acquisition, as children begin to acquire words, build a vocabulary, and then begin to combine words for their first phrases and simple sentences. This is the period of development, therefore, that is the focus of our research.

The Intentionality Model in Figure 3 presents the two components of engagement and effort in interaction with the tripartite model of language *content, form,* and *use* introduced by Bloom and Lahey (1978). Linguistic forms necessarily embody content, or meaning because language is always about something. And language is used differently in different situations according to the circumstances and communication goals of the participants in an exchange, so that form and content articulate with the pragmatics of language use. All three components are required: Language is, necessarily, the *convergence* of content, form, and use. Including language content and use in addition to linguistic form in a model of language ensures that what the child knows and is learning about language at any point in time is intimately connected to other things the child knows and is learning about the social and physical world.

Language will never be acquired without engaging in a world of persons, objects, and events—the world that language is about and in which language is used. The component of *engagement* in the Intentionality Model encompasses the child's emotional and social directedness for determining what is relevant for learning and the motivation for learning. Engagement depends on the psychological dimensions of arousal and responsiveness. From the beginning of life, infants are responsive to other

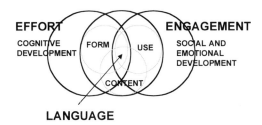

FIGURE 3.—The Intentionality Model.

persons, and the intersubjectivity that develops between infant and care-givers in the first year is the foundation for a child's social connectedness to other persons throughout life (e.g., Emde, 1984; Jaffe, Beebe, Feld-stein, Crown, & Jasnow, 2001; Rogoff, 1990; Stern, 1985). Young children strive to understand what others do and what they say in order to become a part of the social world, but also to interpret the intersecting physical world of objects, movement, relations, and change. Objects ordinarily do not move by themselves; their movements are most often caused by human intervention. This understanding begins in infancy (e.g., Piaget, 1974) and is expressed in early language about causality (Bloom & Cap-atides, 1987a). Engagement, therefore, builds on the intersubjectivity be-tween the child and other persons, and on the relationship between both the child and other persons to the physical world.

The component of *effort* captures the cognitive processes and the work it takes to learn a language. The cognitive resources of the young language-learning child are essentially limited, and learning and using words and sentences for interpretation and expression put demands on those re-sources. At a minimum, learning a word requires the mental representa-tion of an intentional state constructed out of data from perception and memory, associating the word with a component of that representation, and then encoding the word in memory along with its associated contin-gencies. *Expression,* at a minimum, requires the child to construct and hold in mind intentional state representations, retrieve linguistic units and procedures from memory, and articulate the words or sentence. For *interpretation,* at a minimum, the child must connect what is heard to what is already in mind, recall elements from memory that are associated with prior experiences of the words, and form a new intentional state repre-sentation. This new intentional state, in turn, may or may not precipitate the process of expression for saying something in response (see Bloom, Rocissano, & Hood, 1976).

The cognitive processes for learning, interpretation, and expression often operate together, compounding the effort that each requires, because children learn the language in acts of interpretation and expression. More-over, interpretation, expression, and the learning that happens through them occur in connection with emotional responses or other actions and interactions in everyday events. Thus, whatever cognitive resources are available for language learning, expression, and interpretation must be shared and distributed among, at least, emotional responses and expres-sion and learning about objects and relations between them. The effort that these (and other) actions require tends to be overlooked when mech-anisms are invoked to explain language learning that are external to the child—that is, outside of the child's control, such as language acquisition, constraints, devices, genes, and neurological architecture.

Engagement provides the motivation and directedness for development and language learning, and effort ensures that the process goes forward, but engagement and effort do not operate without an essential tension between them. Both development over time and the integration of different behaviors in immediate time depend on an essential tension between effort and engagement in the expression of a young child's intentionality (Bloom, 1993a, 1998). The notion of *essential tension* is attributable to Thomas Kuhn who described the shifts that take place in scientific theory when existing theories resist accommodation of new observations or new facts (Kuhn, 1962, 1977). New theory comes out of the tension that is inevitable when certain observations, certain phenomena, certain facts are *discrepant* (inconsistent or incompatible or otherwise not accounted for) by existing theory.

A succession of theoretical tensions has characterized language acquisition theory in the last two generations as one and then another theoretical perspective emerged in response to new issues, new concerns, or new data. These theoretical tensions began with the challenge to behaviorism (Skinner, 1957) from the theory of generative transformational grammar (Chomsky, 1959) and resulted in the tension between innatist and environmental explanations of language acquisition that continues today (e.g., Pinker, 1994; Tomasello, 1995). In the past two generations, tensions arose between theories with different world views and emphases on general cognition or social interaction or brain function for responding to one or another new observation or fact about language and its acquisition (see Bloom, 1998, 2001).

An essential tension figures in the development of the child, just as it does in the development of theory. Developmental change is not simply quantitative or cumulative: A child does not simply add one ability, skill, or behavior to another to become the mature adult. Nor does the child simply add words or add one syntactic structure to another on the way to the mature language. Developmental change is necessarily directed, and in the case of language acquisition it is directed at the target language. But the process of linguistic change is responsive to the tension that results from discrepancy, when the child's knowledge, including knowledge of language, cannot accommodate new encounters. It is that discrepancy and the tension that results from it that are the real mechanisms of the processes of organization, differentiation, integration, reorganization, and consolidation that underlie developmental change.

These general developmental processes emerge out of an essential tension between the child's engagement in new encounters and the child's effort to connect what is already known to the new information and contradictions presented in such encounters. It is the sort of dialectical tension that is, in fact, required for all of human development (e.g., Bidell, 1988; Overton, 1998). In a dialectical account, contradiction and conflict lead to restructuring and motivate developmental change. This restructuring occurs as a cycle of thesis (an original state or act), antithesis (an inconsistency, or the resistance encountered in acting), and synthesis (a resolution of the inconsistency that includes features of both thesis and antithesis). The child could never develop, could never become a self-sufficient productive adult, without experiencing and working through a succession of such tensions that emerge from the experience of contradiction.

An essential tension is inherent in virtually every theory of human development, from Freud to Erickson to Piaget—to name just three, very different theories—whether it is explicitly acknowledged or not. The tension required for human development was articulated most explicitly by Freud, whose theory was a *tension reduction theory* (e.g., Freud, 1962). In Freud's view, the primordial, initial principle of life comes from the tension between pleasure and pain. This tension led to Freud's articulation of the "pleasure principle" that has as its aim avoiding pain and finding pleasure. Freud pointed out that *there would be no psychological development* if all the infant's tensions could be handled by the reflex mechanisms (blinking, sneezing, coughing, bladder opening) that remove tension-causing physical disturbances. However, for many tensions, such as hunger, there are no reflex mechanisms. Again, there would be no psychological development if parents were able to meet all the child's needs and take care of every tension, an unlikely scenario because parents not only reduce tensions but create them by imposing schedules, training, and discipline for the infant's (and their own) well-being. Freud's theory grows increasingly abstract as it extends to tensions that originate in dynamic processes hidden deep in the individual's unconscious for psychological development.

Piaget's theory of cognitive development (e.g., Piaget, 1952, 1954) came out of an entirely different theoretical agenda but is, nevertheless, implicitly a tension reduction theory (although he, himself, did not call it that). Equilibration, in Piaget's theory, is the analogy of Freud's pleasure principle. For Piaget, disequilibrium occurs when new encounters resist interpretation and understanding—when the information in new encounters is discrepant from what the child already knows and cannot be assimilated to existing knowledge. The dialectical tension that results from the contradiction between the known and the unknown forces a revision in existing knowledge. Again, quite simply, *there would be no cognitive development* without the tension that presses existing forms of thought to change in the effort to accommodate new information.

17

Just as tension is required for psychological development in general and cognitive development in particular, tension is required for developmental change in language acquisition. *There would be no progress in language* without the tension from discrepancy in the mind of the child between existing knowledge and new encounters, and between what the child and other persons have in mind. The tension is productive, in the sense that Piaget describes the child moving toward equilibrium, rather than being a "felt" discomfort in the Freudian account of seeking pleasure and avoiding pain. We have conceptualized the tension required for language acquisition as an *essential tension in the dialectical relation between engagement and effort.* Engagement follows from young children's affective investment in and intersubjectivity with other persons, and their mutual attention and interest in objects and events in the world. However, engagement meets resistance in the effort it takes to overcome the discrepancy between what the child already knows about language and the new language needed to resolve the discrepancy in understanding between the child and other persons.

An essential tension also results when engagement in learning the language meets resistance in the effort to overcome competition for limited cognitive resources that must be shared between language and other behaviors, and between different aspects of development going on at the same time. Resolving the essential tension between engagement and effort is the work of the young child's thinking. The primary empirical assumption in the research reported in this *Monograph* is that evidence of this essential tension and its resolution in the child's mind can be inferred from children's actions, particularly actions of expression and interpretation in the stream of ordinary activities.

Explanatory Principles

Three principles are included in the Intentionality Model for mediating between engagement and effort and resolving the tension between them. They are the principles of relevance, discrepancy, and elaboration (Bloom, 1993a). These principles are generalizations that describe the cognitive transactions between internal representations and the external social and physical world. *Discrepancy* between what the child and others have in mind, and between what the child already knows and input that resists understanding, motivates the effort required to learn and use language. *Relevance* results from the resolution of discrepancy and explains what captures a child's engagement for learning and interaction. *Elaborations* of intentional state representations, as a consequence of developments in both cognition and language, explain the child's movement toward learning and using increasingly more complex and abstract language for expression. These explanatory principles, themselves, are not in the child's mind. They are a heuristic in the model for describing the transactions between internal mental states and external events, and they explain why and how language is acquired.

According to the principle of discrepancy, development is enhanced when children act to resolve a mismatch between what they have in mind and what is already evident from the situation. As infants begin to remember past events and anticipate new events that other persons cannot yet know, clues from the context cannot be exploited for shared understanding. Children have to acquire a language for expression when contents of mind differ from what others have in mind and need to be shared. Support for the principle of discrepancy in prior research comes from the finding that children's talk about events that are anticipated—imminent in the situation but not yet evident—increases when compared to their talk about things already evident (Bloom, Beckwith, Capatides, & Hafitz, 1988). As they learn more words, children talk more about things that have not yet happened and so cannot be known by a listener. Similarly, mothers use verbs that name anticipated, impending actions more often than actions that are already underway (and therefore evident) when interacting with their one-year-old children (Tomasello & Kruger, 1992).

The principle of discrepancy is consistent with the classic observation that children are attracted to novelty in a learning situation (e.g., Fantz, 1964; McCall & McGhee, 1977). Young children's attraction to the novelty in discrepant events has been well exploited in experimental studies of early cognition (e.g., Spelke, 1991) and word learning (e.g., Hirsh-Pasek & Golinkoff, 1996). However, infants attend longer to an event that is similar to but does not quite match a familiar event, than to the familiar event or an entirely new event (the "discrepancy principle" described by Kagan, 1971, p. 62).

According to the principle of relevance, development is enhanced when events in the context bear upon and are pertinent to what the child has in mind. "Relevance is the single property that makes information worth processing and determines the particular assumptions an individual is most likely to construct and process" (Sperber & Wilson, 1986, p. 46). The principle of relevance determines, in particular, the things that prompt a child's attention, interest, and emotional investment in the personal and physical world. The relevance of other persons' behaviors is assured, and their language made accessible for learning, when adults either tune in to what a child is already feeling and thinking or succeed in redirecting the child's focus of attention to new information in a context that might be worth knowing and, therefore, relevant.

Caregivers are clearly sensitive to the principle of relevance in their interactions with young children. Studies of the effects of joint attention and shared understanding, in particular, have shown how language learning is enhanced when child and caregiver share a focus of attention and caregivers talk about what the child is attending to (e.g., Masur, 1982; Tomasello & Akhtar, 1995; Tomasello & Farrar, 1986). Likewise, caregivers are primarily responsive in conversations with young children, picking up on topics that the child initiates more often than introducing new topics (Harris, 1992; Howe, 1981). Children, for their part, are much more likely to initiate topics in early conversations based on what they have in mind than to share a topic from what someone else has just said (Bloom et al., 1976; Bloom et al., 1996). The principle of relevance also applies when caregivers have difficulty understanding an infant's expression and engage in "negotiation," providing the linguistic forms that embody what the child has in mind for recasting the message (Golinkoff, 1986).

According to the principle of elaboration, children will have to learn more of the language for expression and interpretation in order to keep up with developments that enrich the representations in intentional states. Developments in the symbolic capacity, concepts, conceptual structure, and the content and organization of knowledge promote increasingly elaborate and abstract representations in consciousness. The principle of elaboration explains the child acting in increasingly explicit ways to express and articulate the increasing number of elements, roles, and relations between them in intentional states.

By the end of the first year, more explicit forms of expression are required than the affective signals that served the infant so well in the first year of life, so that language has to be learned. On the most general level, evidence for the principle of elaboration is obvious from the considerable advances children make in both vocabulary and the complexity of their syntax in the preschool years, coextensive with developments in other aspects of cognition. In the single-word period in the second year, in particular, children's talk about anticipated action events, with more elements and relations between elements, increases compared to talk about objects in stative, presentational events. This development prefigures the subsequent transition to phrases and simple sentences (Bloom, Beckwith, Capatides, & Hafitz, 1988). As shown in the earlier study of children's play by Lifter and Bloom (1989), more elaborated constructions with more roles and relations between objects develop later than earlier constructions that consist only of putting one object into or on top of another object.

In sum, the principles of relevance, discrepancy, and elaboration describe three characteristics of the relation between internal mental states and external events that explain why language begins and why acquisition moves forward toward the language of the community of mature language users. *Relevance* is the meaningfulness of external events to internal, mental events; *discrepancy* is the disjunction in mental events between what is known already and what is unknown to the child, or between the child and other persons; and *elaboration* is the qualitative richness of mental contents that demands a corresponding richness of language for expression and interpretation.

TESTING THE INTENTIONALITY MODEL

Intentional states are the continuously changing representations in mind that are expressed by actions in the flow of everyday events. In order to test the hypotheses of engagement and effort and the tension between them, the purpose of the studies reported in this *Monograph* was to examine how different expressions—children's speech, emotion, and play with objects, along with their mothers' speech (on the assumption that children interpret mothers' speech to them)—occur *in relation to each other in the stream of activity*. Expressions were examined in both the real time of ordinary activities and the developmental time encompassed by three reference points in language acquisition: first words, a vocabulary spurt, and the transition to sentences. The new research reported here continues the program of longitudinal research into aspects of the children's expressions described in previous publications, and that earlier research is reviewed here as background before the general hypotheses and expectations for the new studies are presented.

Previous Research to Test the Model

Three quantitative analyses of emotional expression in relation to vocabulary acquisition have been reported. In a study of chronological developments at ages 9, 13, 17, and 21 months, children who were earlier and later word learners were compared with respect to the valence and intensity of their affect expressions. Although the two subgroups of earlier and later learners did not differ at age 9 months, frequency of emotional expression increased from 9 to 17 months for the children who were later word learners but remained stable for the earlier word learners (Bloom, Beckwith, & Capatides, 1988). Thus, later learners increased their emotional expressivity as they grew older instead of learning language early. However, in a second study (Bloom, Beckwith, Capatides, & Hafitz, 1988), instead of comparison according to chronological age, frequency of emotional expression was compared between two developments in vocabulary: between appearance of the first words and the sharp increase in acquisition of new words termed the *vocabulary spurt*. Emotional expression did not change for the group of children as a whole between the two developments in language, even though the later learners had increased in their emotional expression in relation to chronological age.

In another study, different aspects of emotional expression at first words and vocabulary spurt were correlated with age at the time of first words and at vocabulary spurt. Frequency of emotional expression was positively correlated with age at first words and vocabulary spurt, and frequency of emotional expression at vocabulary spurt was positively correlated with age of transition to saying sentences. Thus, the children who expressed emotion more frequently were also older at the time of these language developments. The corollary was that time spent in neutral affect was negatively correlated with age of language developments, with earlier learners spending more time in neutral affect (Bloom & Capatides, 1987b). Thus, later word learners both expressed emotion more frequently than earlier word learners and increased in their emotional expression in relation to chronological age, but were nevertheless stable in their expression of emotion between first word acquisition and vocabulary spurt.

The most direct test of the Intentionality Model was an earlier study of the propositional content and psychological attitudes of belief and desire that could be attributed to the intentional states expressed by speech and emotional expression (Bloom, Beckwith, Capatides, & Hafitz, 1988; also see Bloom, 1994). Desires were expressed more frequently than beliefs by both emotional expression and words, and desires were most often about the child's actions rather than desires for their mothers to do something. Emotion was the dominant form of expression at first words, as expected. At the vocabulary spurt, words expressed the majority of propositions in all categories except the category of belief. Beliefs involving other persons and their actions toward the child continued to be expressed with emotion more than words. Expression of meanings about dynamic action increased in comparison with static, presentational kinds of meanings with a focus on only a single object. Meanings about action entailed multiple elements, roles, and relations between them, so that their increase in the single-word period supports the principle of elaboration. In addition, most of the children's words expressed meanings that were already evident, in the sense that they were directed to present objects and or events in progress. However, *anticipated* expression about imminent events increased from first words to vocabulary spurt, and this increase in expression of anticipated events was greater with dynamic action content than stative content. Thus, the principle of discrepancy was supported in the development of intentional state contents that could not otherwise be known to a listener because they were anticipated by the child, imminent but not yet evident.

22

The children's spontaneous play with objects was examined for evidence of developments in object knowledge in three developmental windows related to language: the prespeech period at ages 9, 10, and 11 months; the three-month window around first words; and the three-month window around the vocabulary spurt (reported in Lifter & Bloom, 1989). Two kinds of object displacements were identified, separations and constructions, with subcategories of constructions then identified according to the kind of thematic relations constructed between the objects. Separations predominated initially; the emergence of constructions occurred in the prespeech period. Achievement in constructions was associated with first words, and constructions continued to increase from first words to vocabulary spurt. The earliest thematic constructions were either reproductions of the original relations in which the children were presented with the objects (given relations) or general relations of containment or support (putting one object into or on top of another with no other thematic content). The development of specific thematic relations (constructions that took into account other perceptual and cultural properties of the objects) was more strongly associated with the vocabulary spurt at the end of the single-word period than with chronological age. Thus, development of the more elaborated specific constructions between objects together with the vocabulary spurt in word learning provided support for the principle of elaboration.

A form of lag sequential analysis was developed to examine speech and emotional expression occurring in relation to each other in real time, at first words and at vocabulary spurt, by Bloom and Beckwith (1989). That study is summarized below as the prototype (the "Background Study") for the analyses reported in this *Monograph*, because the procedures as well as the results of both the Transition to Sentences Study and the Play Study refer back to the original study. The lag sequential analysis was also used to study the patterns of conversational turn-taking between the children and their mothers at first words and vocabulary spurt by Bloom et al. (1996). Measured against their respective baseline rates of speech, children were most likely to talk before mother speech and mothers most likely to talk after child speech; both child and mother were least likely to be talking at the same time. This pattern of turn-taking showed significantly greater excursions from baseline rates at vocabulary spurt than at first words. Only about one third of all child speech occurred in response to something mothers said. Mothers' responses were most often acknowledgements, repetitions, or clarifications of what a child said rather than other kinds of topic-related response or a new topic. We concluded, therefore, that the conversations between the children and their mothers in this naturalistic playroom context were driven primarily by what the child had in mind, as the children took the lead in initiating the topics of conversation most often, and mothers supported both the child's topic and the interaction by responding promptly.

The research in this *Monograph* builds on this program of longitudinal research with the same group of 12 infants. Two new studies are reported here. First, the Transition to Sentences Study is an extension of the original study of emotional expression and speech at first words and vocabulary spurt (Bloom & Beckwith, 1989) to the later time in development marked by the children's transition to saying phrases and simple sentences. Second, the principal research in the *Monograph*, the Play Study, is a continuation of the study of the children's object play with examination of speech and emotional expression in the moments before, during, and after the children constructed thematic relations between objects. The lag sequential procedures were used here with the children's object constructions (as coded by Lifter & Bloom, 1989) as the *target events*, in order to examine the contingency of other expressive actions in relation to actions in object play and in relation to each other in the context of object play.

For the purposes of the studies reported in this *Monograph*, the transcriptions of the children's speech and coded data used in the previous studies of emotional expression and object play were reviewed and verified by independent coders. These transcription and coding procedures are described below. In the Play Study, the moment-to-moment temporal patterns of the several different expressive actions in immediate time were also compared across time developmentally, at first words and at vocabulary spurt, to determine how emergence and achievements in both language and play influenced the temporal patterns of expression. The children's later play at the transition to sentences could not be included in these analyses because children's play with objects has not been coded after the vocabulary spurt.

In sum, the research in the present study continued a larger program of longitudinal research into the development of a group of 12 infants, beginning at age 9 months and continuing through the emergence of words at, on average, age 13 months; the development of a basic vocabulary in the second year; and the beginning of sentences at, on average, age 24 months. Having already reported developments in these children's early word learning, affect expression, object play, and conversational interactions separately, we now show how these different expressive actions came together in both immediate time, as activities unfolded in the ordinary, spontaneous events in the playroom, and in the extended time encompassed by developmental reference points in language in the second year of life: first words, a time of transition and emergence, and the vocabulary spurt, a time of consolidation and achievement in word learning. Studying expressive behaviors at times of developmental transition, with emergence and achievement in both language and play, provided an opportunity to observe the effects of the tension between engagement and effort and its resolution for development. The temporal relation between speech and emotional expression was also examined at a second transition and time of emergence, the onset of phrases and simple sentences.

General Hypotheses and Expectations in the Present Research

The two principal hypotheses for the research were based on the fundamental theoretical constructs that informed the Intentionality Model, effort and engagement, and the tension that was expected between them.

Hypothesis of Effort

Distribution of effort is necessary when attending to more than one task at the same time: "Because the total quantity of effort which can be exerted at any one time is limited, concurrent activities which require attention tend to interfere with one another" (Kahneman, 1973, p. 12). Dual task experiments with adults and children have shown that performance on one task diminishes when attention is turned to another task (e.g., see Bjorklund & Harnishfeger, 1990, and Guttentag, 1989, for reviews). In the natural "experiment" provided by our playroom for observing children's spontaneous everyday behaviors, their speech (in the Transition to Sentences Study) or their constructions with objects (in the Play Study) were considered the target task they performed, and other behaviors were examined in the seconds before, during, and after these target behaviors. Emotional expression was examined relative to speech in the Transition to Sentences Study, and child speech, child emotional expressions, and mother speech were examined relative to object constructions, and each other, in the Play Study.

A key issue in studies of dual task performance is whether behaviors tap into a single, general purpose resource pool, as was suggested by Kahneman (1973), or into multiple, somewhat independent resources, depending on the nature of the task, as suggested, for example, by Just and Carpenter (1992). In the research reported in this *Monograph*, if one kind of behavior does not deviate from its expected probability of occurrence when observed in the context of a different kind of behavior, then we might conclude that the two are independent of each other and draw on separate resource pools. However, as the earlier study reported by Bloom and Beckwith (1989) demonstrated, emotional expression is not independent of children's speech. Emotional expression in that study varied systematically in its deviation from baseline around the children's words, thus suggesting that the two forms of expression share resources from a single pool.

The general expectation for the occurrence of multiple behaviors in real time, in the studies reported here, is that frequency of emotional expression will not be independent but will continue to covary around speech at the time of the transition to sentences, and that child speech, child emotional expression, and mother speech will covary systematically in their occurrence around object play. More specifically, we hypothesize that different behaviors occurring together in the same window of time express aspects of the same intentional states and, therefore, draw on the same pool of resources with a consequent cost to the child in cognitive effort. The first expectation based on this hypothesis, in the Play Study below, is that saying words and expressing emotion will diminish in the moments around constructing a thematic relation between objects as a result of the effort that each kind of behavior required.

However, although different behaviors may draw on the same pool of resources, developments in the second year of life can be expected in (a) cognitive capacity, (b) the relative cognitive requirements of different behaviors, and (c) access to the cognitive resources that behaviors require. Therefore, the covariation among different behaviors may, itself, be expected to vary with development over time. Because "novel stimuli, in particular, are favored in the allocation of capacity" (Kahneman, 1973, p. 42), something else has to give when the essentially limited resources of the young language-learning child are allocated to new learning. The developmental expectation in the research reported in this *Monograph* is that learning language (as marked by the transitions to saying words and then sentences) and learning about objects (by constructing different thematic relations between objects in play) will preempt the resources that other, earlier developing behaviors (emotional expression) might draw on at the same time. Therefore, greater effort is expected with new learning—that is, at times of emergence and transition in language acquisition (at first words and the transition to sentences)—than at times of consolidation and achievement in learning (at vocabulary spurt).

The second expectation, in the Play Study, is that the reduction of expressive behaviors will be greater relative to baseline at first words than at vocabulary spurt. The third expectation, in the Transition to Sentences Study, is that the effort of learning syntax and making the transition to sentences will result in the reduction of emotional expression relative to baseline around speech, even though emotional expression was not reduced around speech at vocabulary spurt in the previous study by Bloom and Beckwith (1989).

26

Hypothesis of Engagement and the Tension Between Effort and Engagement

The level of engagement that a child brings to a task is determined by the extent to which the child finds the task interesting (Renninger, 1990; Renninger & Wozniak, 1985), important, and relevant or "worth knowing" (Sperber & Wilson, 1986). Engagement for language learning is closely tied to a child's investment in (a) intersubjectivity between self and other, for resolving discrepancy between what each has in mind and sharing contents of mind, and (b) learning about the physical world, for resolving the discrepancy between what is already known and new encounters that resist understanding. Thus, engagement is characterized by approach, valuation, and feelings directed toward other persons and toward novelty in the physical world. Engagement is evident in the well-known tendency infants have to attend and respond with positive affect to relatively novel events in preference to events that are either already familiar or beyond their understanding (McCall & McGhee, 1977).

Emotional expressions are an index of engagement and evidence of arousal. In the research reported here, emotional expressions were coded as positively and negatively valenced affect expression relative to neutral, nonemotionally valenced affect. The assumption is that an increase in engagement can be inferred from heightened emotional expression relative to baseline. And, indeed, emotional expression did increase considerably above its baseline level during and immediately after saying words at vocabulary spurt in the original study reported by Bloom and Beckwith (1989). This finding led to the conclusion that children are learning to talk about those things that are relevant to them and, therefore, interesting as the objects of their engagement. The absence of change in emotional expression relative to baseline would not, however, indicate a lack of engagement but only engagement at its average (i.e., baseline) level.

As evidence of arousal, emotional expression ties the concept of engagement to the arousal component in a model of effort: "the key observation that variations in physiological arousal accompany variations in effort shows that the limited capacity and the arousal system must be closely related . . . both increase or decrease according to the changing demands of current activities" (Kahneman, 1973, p. 10). The relation of arousal to decreases in performance has been documented in experiments with animals and humans since the beginning of the last century: "Task performance [decreases] with increasing arousal . . . [and] this decrement occurs sooner in complex tasks than in simple ones" (Kahneman, p. 37, citing Easterbrook, 1959, and others). These observations led to the expectation, in the present study, that emotional expression will preempt performance in other tasks. The earlier research with the same group of children (Bloom & Capatides, 1987b) may be understood as partial support for this expectation. There, the discovered correlations between affect expression and language learning are consistent with the interpretation that frequent emotional expression interfered with learning language early, and more time in neutral affect promoted earlier language learning.

Emotional displays entail *cognitive activity* for the mentally represented content that they express. Additionally, emotional experience and its expression entail cognitive appraisals and valuations of circumstances in a situation relative to a mental goal (e.g., Arnold, 1960; Mandler, 1984). Given these relations between cognition and emotion, emotional expression should be sensitive to the effort and cognitive resources expended on other actions. Another interpretation of the earlier results reported by Bloom and Capatides (1987b), therefore, has to do with competition for scarce resources: Children who were earlier word learners may have expressed more neutral affect and less emotion because of the effort required for early language learning; children who started learning words later were able to express more emotion instead. Thus, bidirectional effects between emotional expression and other actions could be expected as one of the consequences of the tension between engagement and effort. Emotional expression might either be diminished or enhanced relative to baseline, according to the relative degree of both engagement and effort invested in a concomitant task.

In the research reported in this *Monograph*, an increase in emotional expression relative to baseline levels is interpreted as evidence of heightened arousal and engagement in the relative absence of effort. A decrease in emotional expression and suppression of arousal is interpreted to indicate either diminished engagement, with less interest in a task, or the expenditure of effort preempting a child's resources. Considering both (a) emotional expression as an index of engagement and (b) the reduction of emotional expression relative to baseline levels as a reflection of effort, children will be expected to express more emotion relative to baseline with *achievement* or mastery in language (at vocabulary spurt) than with *emergence* of new learning (at first words and the transition to sentences). In addition, in the Play Study, engagement is expected to be reflected in heightened emotional expression relative to baseline in the context of constructing specific relations between objects that represent achievement in more recent learning, and less emotional expression in the context of constructing the earlier learned, familiar, given relations.

Finally, two conflicting expectations influenced expectations about mothers' speech to their children in the context of play with objects. Research and theory in the literature that describes the role of "scaffolding" and "guided learning" (e.g., Bruner, 1983a, 1983b; Ninio & Bruner, 1978; Rogoff, 1993; Tomasello, 1992; Vygotsky, 1962, 1978) would indicate that one could expect mothers to take the lead in directing their children's constructing activities with objects. On the one hand, if mothers are, indeed, scaffolding and guiding the children's play with the toys and learning through constructing activities, we expect them to be most likely to talk in the moments before or during the constructing activity. On the other hand, mothers were primarily responsive as the children took the lead in their conversations in the previous study of conversational interaction (Bloom et al., 1996). Therefore, an alternative expectation in the study reported here is that mothers will be primarily responsive as well in the context of the children's play, talking more relative to their baseline rates of talking in the moments immediately after rather than before or during the constructions.

In sum, the questions addressed in the research reported in this *Monograph* have to do with (a) the moment-to-moment temporal contingencies, in immediate time, between saying words and expressing emotion at the time of transition to sentences, and among saying words, expressing emotion, and attending to mothers' speech in relation to actions in play, and (b) changes in the patterns of these contingencies over time with developments in both language and object play in the second year. Hypotheses based on the concepts of effort, engagement, and the essential tension between them guided the expectations in this research. First, emotional expression is expected to decrease around speech in the Transition to Sentences Study because of the effort required at times of emergence and transition for new language learning, even though we expect that children continue to talk about objects of engagement (as inferred from their heightened emotional expression at the vocabulary spurt, a time of achievement rather than emergence). Second, based on the hypothesis of effort in the Play Study, object play, speech, emotional expression, and interpreting mothers' speech are expected to compete with each other for limited cognitive resources, resulting in reciprocal increase and decrease in the different expressive behaviors. And based on the hypothesis of engagement and the greater investment that children have in achievement in new learning, emotional expression is expected to increase with construction of the more advanced specific constructions that were achieved at vocabulary spurt.

Two new studies are reported. The first, the Transition to Sentences Study, extends the analyses of the temporal patterns of child emotional expression during and around speech to the transition to saying phrases and simple sentences. The research that is the primary focus of this *Monograph*—the Play Study—is based on the subset of all the activities recorded in the playroom in which the children acted on two objects to create a thematic relation between them. Temporal contingencies between child and mother expressive behaviors are examined in relation to the children's object play in immediate time, and in relation to developments in object play over time, at first words and at the vocabulary spurt.

THE CHILDREN AND THEIR MOTHERS

The children in this study were 6 girls and 6 boys, all first born and living in the greater New York metropolitan area. Eight children were Euro-American; 2 were African-American; 1 both African-American and Puerto Rican Hispanic; and 1 was Dominican Hispanic, Euro-American, and Native American. These last 4 children were also from the poorest families in our sample (with incomes less than $10,000 in 1982). Except for non-English kin terms, for example, Hebrew "Aba" and "Ema" and occasional Spanish words like "agua" and "mira!," American English and the African-American English vernacular were spoken in their homes. All of the mothers were their children's primary caregivers throughout the study, and none was working outside the home when the study was begun. (See Bloom, 1993a, for further description of the children and their development in this period of time.)

DATA COLLECTION

The children and their mothers visited our playroom at Teachers College, Columbia University, every month, beginning when the children were

9 months of age and continuing until they were saying simple sentences at about 2 years of age, on average. These monthly 1-hr observations were video-recorded and augmented by monthly video-recorded home visits until the children were 15 months old, and then every 3 months thereafter. The monthly observations were also augmented by diaries the mothers kept of their children's progress in word learning. (The home visits and mother diaries were used for supplementary information; the research reported here was based only on the video-recorded playroom observations.) The same pair of research assistants responsible for collecting the monthly data in the playroom also visited the children at home, and these research assistants were in touch by telephone with the mothers in the weeks between sessions. The children and the research assistants were matched for race.

The mothers were asked to play with their infants in the playroom as they might ordinarily play with them at home. The playroom was equipped with a child-sized table and two chairs, a 3-ft plastic slide with a crawl space, and a changing table. A group of toys was on the floor when the infant and mother entered the playroom, and other groups of toys were brought in every 8 minutes according to a schedule. A snack instead of a new group of toys was provided after the first half hour. The selection of toys was balanced so that the children had equal time for both manipulative and enactment play; for example, a set of plastic nesting cups is a manipulative toy and rubber farm animals are enactment toys. In addition, because traditionally gender-stereotyped toys might have different appeal to boys and girls, we provided equal time for the children to play with traditional girl toys (e.g., the baby doll), boy toys (e.g., the dump truck), and neutral toys (e.g., the nesting cups).

The same toys were presented every month, on the same schedule, to all the children. This consistency in the situation in which we observed the children provided a measure of confidence for assuming that change in a child's behaviors and in the interactions between child and mother over time can be attributed to development, and that differences between the child-mother pairs can be attributed to inherent differences among them rather than to the setting in which we observed them.

The mother-infant interactions were video recorded using Sony SLO-383 half-inch stereo Betamax interfaced with a FOR-A 3500 SMPTE time-code generator. The computer-readable time code was a discrete audio signal recorded every 1/30th s on the second sound track of the video tape to mark 30 frames/s. At the time of data processing, the videodeck was interfaced with an Apple II plus microprocessor via a time code reader for coding and transcription (see Beckwith, Bloom, Albury, Raqib, & Booth, 1985; Bloom, 1993b).

Mothers' speech and the children's speech, emotional expressions, and play activities were each transcribed and coded by different persons

31

who were unaware of the purposes of the present study. They each worked independently, while viewing and coding from the video record, to create separate files for each of the variables in the study. Every transcription entry and coding decision was associated with a time of behavior onset and offset. The time codes for onset and offset of child and mother speech, emotional expression, and object play made it possible for the computer to integrate the separate files and thereby restore the original temporal sequence in which the behaviors occurred.

PROCEDURES

Equating the Children for Language Development

Children differ widely in age of onset and rate of language acquisition (e.g., as summarized in Shore, 1995). Accordingly, the children were equated on the basis of progress in language acquisition rather than age for examining the temporal contingencies between linguistic and other kinds of behavior and changes in those contingencies over time. Three developmental reference points in language were identified: first words, vocabulary spurt, and the transition to sentences. These reference points allowed us to look at changes in the temporal contingencies between behaviors as a function of developmental transition and change rather than simply age (see Connell and Furman, 1984, and Emde and Harmon, 1984, for justification of using times of transition in development for analyses in longitudinal research).

The emergence of first words was identified when a child first said at least one phonetically consistent, meaningful, conventional word at least two separate times in the playroom. The words the children said in the playroom sessions were transcribed every month and a record was kept of the new words the children learned each month. The vocabulary spurt was identified when the slope of the increase in new words in the playroom included at least 12 new words after 20 words had already been acquired. (See Bloom, 1993a, p. 147, for details of the rationale and procedures for identifying these language developments.) The criterion of saying a word at least twice was used only to identify first words, and not for identifying the vocabulary spurt. The criterion of 12 new words in a month after at least 20 words had already been learned was not arbitrary; it was based on the parameters that characterized a change in the slope of the vocabulary growth curve of the 3 children studied by Lifter (1982) who provided the pilot data for the larger study. Some investigators (e.g., Goldfield & Reznick, 1990) have questioned whether all children show a vocabulary spurt, and the issue has since been debated in the literature. However, for the purposes of the research reported here, the three ref-

32

erence points provide a convenient index for equating the children and comparing their developments in language to other developments at the same time.

First words was a time of *emergence* and transition, when the children first began to say words in the playroom (mean number of different words, 4.7; range, 2–12 words). The vocabulary spurt was a time of *achievement* and consolidation in word learning, after having learned a substantial number of words (mean number of words, 51; range, 34–75 words). Beginning to say phrases and simple sentences was another *transition* and was identified when a child's mean length of utterance reached 1.5 words, a commonly used criterion for establishing the beginning of syntactic speech.

Mean ages for the 12 children at the three language milestones, respectively, were first words at 13 months 26 days (range = 10 months 5 days to 17 months 23 days); vocabulary spurt at 19 months 7 days (range = 13 months 2 days to 25 months 6 days); and sentences at 23 months 7 days (range = 17 months 4 days to 28 months 3 days). All the children had reached a 50-word cumulative vocabulary in the playroom within 1 month of the month in which they met the criteria for a vocabulary spurt (either in the same month or 1 month before or after). The children's mean ages at all of these milestones was consistent with virtually all other studies of early developments in vocabulary and syntax.

Data Coding

Speech transcription. The children's speech at first words, at vocabulary spurt, and at transition to sentences was first transcribed by hand and then verified by a second transcriber who entered the data into the computer with times of speech onset and offset. The computer record was then reviewed by both transcribers together to resolve any disagreements between the two transcription passes; if agreement was not reached, the utterance was entered in phonetic notation as a nonword and not included in subsequent analyses. The average margin of error among coders for coding speech onset and offset times (after extensive training) was remarkably small: within 2 video frames (or $1/15$ s) for word onset, and within 5 video frames (or $1/6$ s) for word offset (Bloom & Beckwith, 1989). The mothers' speech was transcribed independently, by different transcribers, in the same way. Subsequently, approximately 3 to 5 years later, the mother and child observations and transcriptions were reviewed again by another research team to verify and edit the computer entries to allow for different computer analyses (e.g., Bloom et al., 1993, 1996) and the research reported in this *Monograph*.

Emotional expression. With the basic assumption that affect is always present normally, children's affect expressions were coded continuously in the stream of activity, so that every shift in affect expression and the duration of all expressions were captured. Coding was based at the level of description, using the gradient information of valence (hedonic tone) and intensity (Bloom, Beckwith, & Capatides, 1988; Bloom & Capatides, 1987b; see Adamson & Bakeman, 1982; Ricciuti & Poresky, 1972; and Stechler & Carpenter, 1967). The coding categories for valence were neutral, negative, positive, mixed, and equivocal hedonic tone, with three levels of intensity indicating the relative fullness of a display (see Bloom, 1993a, for photograph examples of these different categories of expression).

Neutral expression was defined by the face being in a resting or baseline position, without movement, as described by Ekman and Friesen (1978), and without body tension or affective vocalization. An emotional expression was defined as any observable shift from neutral to nonneutral valence and/or shift in intensity as coded from a child's facial expression, body tension or posture, and/or affective vocalizations (whining, laughing, and the like). Mixed affect expression included elements of both positive and negative valence; equivocal affect was neither positive, negative, nor neutral, as happened with expressions of surprise or excitement.

Every shift in expressed affect was identified and entered into the computer with its time of onset. The frame before the onset time of the next shift in affect expression was the offset time of the preceding expression. The result was a continuous record of affect expressions and their duration from one shift in expression to another. The average margin of error among coders for coding affect onset time (after extensive training) was 16 video frames or approximately $1/2$ s. This was somewhat greater than the onset and offset times for speech due to the fact that several kinds of continuous cues were used to code affect (facial expression, body tension, affective vocalization). Subsequently, approximately 3 to 5 years later, all the coding for affect expression was reviewed to verify and edit the computer entries for other research (reported in Capatides, 1990; Capatides & Bloom, 1993).

Thus, we took a pretheoretical stance in developing a descriptive coding scheme for emotional expressions rather than identifying the discrete emotions (anger, fear, joy, sadness, and the like), although coding the discrete emotions remains an option for future research. This decision is validated by reports that expression of the discrete emotions is, indeed, relatively infrequent in the stream of everyday activity, at least for the age range we studied (e.g., Malatesta, Culver, Tesman, & Shepard, 1989; Phillips & Sellito, 1990). In contrast, shifts in the valence and intensity of children's affect expressions were relatively frequent (Bloom, Beckwith, and Capatides, 1988).

Time spent in expression. The total time spent in speech and emotional expression is shown, in Figure 4, as the percentage of all video frames

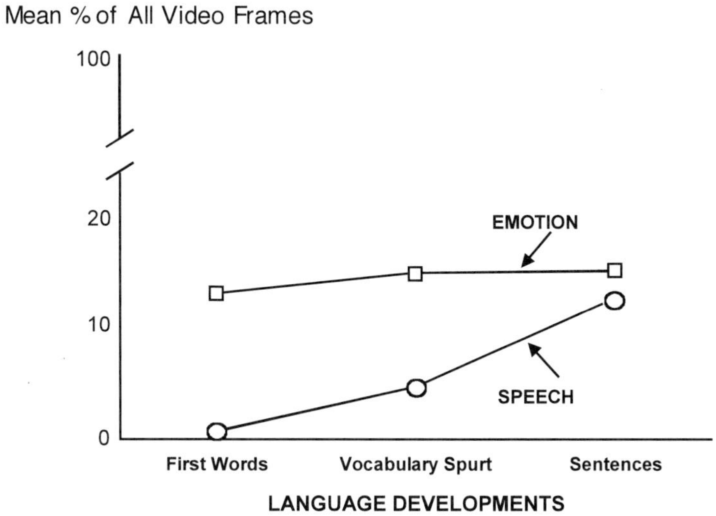

Mean % of All Video Frames

FIGURE 4.—Time spent speaking and expressing emotion shown as the mean percentage of all video frames (1 frame = 1/30th s) in which each kind of expression occurred, all children.

(1 s = 30 frames) in which speech or emotional expression occurred at first words, at vocabulary spurt, and at sentences. The increase in time spent talking was expected, since speech time should increase as children learn and say more words (in the interval between first words and vocabulary spurt) and learn to put words together to form phrases and simple sentences. The developmental increase in percentage of time the children spent speaking was significant, $F(2,18) = 43.054$, $p < .001$.

In contrast, however, emotional expression was stable from first words to sentences, consistent with the findings between first words and vocabulary spurt reported by Bloom, Beckwith, Capatides, and Hafitz (1988) using frequency of expression (number of shifts in valence and/or intensity) as the dependent variable. The stability in emotional expression has two implications: first, the acquisition of language in the second year of life is not simply a manifestation of an overall increase in expressivity, in general. If that were the case, then time spent expressing emotion would have increased along with the increase in time spent talking. In addition, we could conclude that language acquisition did not replace emotional expression. Saying words was not something the children did instead of expressing emotion, since emotional expression in the same period of time did not decrease as speech increased. Rather, the children continued to express emotion as they learned the language for articulating what their emotions were about.

35

Lag Sequential Analysis

A form of lag sequential analysis was used to examine the temporal contingencies between two or more different kinds of behavior in relation to each other. Either child speech (in the Transition to Sentences Study) or object constructions (in the Play Study) were the target events in the analyses. The computer (a) located the onset and offset of a target event in a child's data file in the first half hour of the playroom sessions; then (b) searched for a second, expressive behavior (the "lagged behavior" relative to the target: either child speech, child emotional expression, or mother speech, separately) in each of fifteen 1-s intervals before onset of every target and fifteen 1-s intervals following target offset; and (c) tallied the behaviors that occurred in each 1-s interval. The result of this tally is the frequency of the expressive behavior in each of the 1-s intervals before and after all the targets. These frequencies were then used to determine the *observed incidence of expression* computed as the percentage of all the targets (e.g., the percentage of all the specific constructions) for which a particular kind of expression occurred in each 1-s interval—that is, in the first, second, third, and so forth to the fifteenth 1-s intervals before and then after a target.

The incidence of expression during the target interval itself was treated differently because the duration of a word or construction is typically either longer or shorter than the 1-s intervals before onset or after offset. The likelihood that expression will occur during a target is, therefore, confounded by the duration of the target. Expressions are more likely to occur during targets lasting more than 1 s than in the intervals preceding or following, just because the target happens to be longer than 1 s. Conversely, expressions are less likely to occur during targets lasting less than 1 s. The program corrected for this confound by computing the percentage of the target time (in frames, each 1 s of video tape consisting of 30 frames) in which the lagged behavior was coded. The observed frequency of expression—child speech, child emotion, and mother speech—during each target interval and in each 1-s interval before and after targets was then compared to its expected frequency, the baseline rate of that kind of expression.

Baseline rates of expression. In order to compare the observed incidence of a behavior to its expected probability of occurrence, baseline rates were computed in a way comparable to the method for computing the incidence of observed behaviors and, therefore, differently for target intervals and the 1-s intervals before and after the targets. The baseline for the 1-s intervals before and after targets was the likelihood that an expression would occur in any 1-s interval in the observation—in effect, the percentage of all 1,800 1-s intervals (the first half hour of the observation) in which that kind of expression was coded. The target baseline was the likelihood that an expression would occur during any frame in an observation and was computed as a percentage of all 54,000 frames (the first half hour of the observation) in which the lagged behavior was coded.

In an ad hoc analysis, results were compared using the same baseline rate for both the targets and the 1-s intervals before and after. When targets were treated as a constant, z scores for targets with an average duration less than 1 s were lower than the z scores obtained with the target length treated as variable, because expression was less likely to occur during intervals less than 1 s long. For targets with an average duration longer than 1 s, z scores were higher when the targets were treated the same as the preceding and following 1-s lags only because expressions were more likely to occur during targets longer than 1 s. These results confirmed that we were making the correct adjustment for the variable duration of target events.

Derived z scores were computed for each child for the *observed incidence of expression* in all the target intervals and all the first, second, third, and so forth 1-s intervals before and after all targets. The z scores represented the differences from the baseline in standard deviation units. The formula used for the derived z scores was the mean percentage of the observed expression in an interval, minus the baseline, divided by the standard deviation.

The results reported here consist of the occurrence of (a) emotional expression during, and in the 1-s intervals before and after child speech at the time of emergence of syntax, the Transition to Sentences Study, and (b) child speech, child emotional expressions, and mother speech during, and in the 1-s intervals before and after object constructions in play, at two times in the development of word learning in the second year: at first words, a time of emergence and transition, and at vocabulary spurt, a time of achievement and consolidation in word learning, the Play Study. Temporal patterns among different expressions in relation to each other provide a test of the hypothesis of effort and distribution of resources in both immediate time and developmentally. If expressive behaviors do not deviate from their respective baseline rates in the moments around target events, then we would have to assume that the target activity does not impinge on the distribution of resources for expressive actions. Thus, comparing the incidence of expressions around target events to baseline rates for different kinds of expression allows us to test the null hypothesis of the independence model of effort: Target actions (child speech or object play) will not make a difference in the occurrence of expressive behaviors, and different kinds of expression will not be related to each other. Comparing temporal patterns of expression between times of transition (first words or sentences) and developmental achievement (the vocabulary spurt in word learning and constructing specific thematic relations between objects) provides a test of the hypotheses of engagement (in the achievement of learning) and the essential tension between engagement and effort.

Background Study: Emotional Expression and Speech at First Words and Vocabulary Spurt

The original study of the temporal relation between child emotional expression and child speech during the single-word period (reported in Bloom and Beckwith, 1989) was the prototype for the procedures used in the new studies presented here. The new findings we now report have to be interpreted in light of the results from that earlier study of the children's emotional expressions around speech at first words and at vocabulary spurt. We began with the null hypothesis: If emotional expression and speech are unrelated to each other, then the incidence of one relative to the other should be random because saying words should not interfere with or otherwise influence expressing emotion. The rate of emotional expression before, during, and after saying words should not differ from baseline levels of expressing emotion overall, and patterns of temporal relation should not differ between the two developments in language. The findings, however, demonstrated that emotional expression does vary from baseline relative to saying words, and the variation was systematic not random. Further, the results demonstrated differences at the times of the two language developments, as shown in Figure 5.

The vertical line in Figure 5 represents the time interval of the speech target event, from the onset of a word to the offset of the word (words lasted .91 s, on average). Although the lag sequential analyses used the 15 s before and after the targets, the results were evident in the 5 s immediately before and after. Thus, deviations from baseline clustered around the target. The data points (z-scores) in this and subsequent figures, therefore, are presented relative to baseline for the target interval and only the five 1-s intervals before onset and after offset of the target. These analyses were performed for each child individually relative to that child's own baseline of expressing emotion, before the individual z-scores were averaged for the purpose of the display in Figure 5 (and the figures to follow). The horizontal line in Figure 5, therefore, represents the average of the different baseline rates for the group of 12 children, at first words and at vocabulary spurt.

The data points are standardized z-scores for the differences from baseline in each 1-s interval before and after the target, and the target

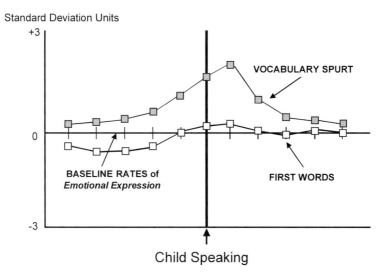

Standard Deviation Units

FIGURE 5.—Temporal pattern of child emotional expression around speech at first words and vocabulary spurt (differences from baseline rates in standard deviation units). (Adapted from Bloom & Beckwith, 1989.)

interval (the vertical line), averaged for the group of 12 children. Scores above the baseline level indicate that emotion was expressed more than expected. Scores below the baseline indicate that emotion was expressed less than expected and the children were, therefore, more likely to be expressing neutral affect.

The results shown in Figure 5 provide evidence of both engagement and effort, and the tension between them, as described in the Intentionality Model. The temporal patterns (the shape of the curves around speech) were the same at both first words and vocabulary spurt. Emotional expression was most likely to occur during words and in the 1-s interval immediately after, indicating *engagement.* The children were learning to talk, in general, about what they cared about, those things that were the objects of their emotional experience and relevant to them.

However, the children expressed significantly less emotion relative to baseline around speech at first words, when they were just learning their earliest words, than at vocabulary spurt, the time of consolidation in word learning, suggesting the effort that the transition to words required. Also, at first words the dip in emotional expression below baseline before speech suggested that the two systems of expression were competing for cognitive resources in the moments of planning prior to saying words, and the effort of planning dampened the tendency to express emotion at the same

39

time. By the time the children reached vocabulary spurt, saying words presumably required less effort, so that the children were able to integrate the two kinds of expression more readily.

Even though emotional expression and speech appear to be integrated at vocabulary spurt, the two forms of expression come together only with certain constraints that indicate the effort they still require. As reported by Bloom and Beckwith (1989), the words said with emotion are the words that presumably are "easier" (i.e., the children's most frequent and/or earliest learned words). Emotion is less likely to be expressed with new presumably "harder" words. Moreover, the emotion they express at the same time as speech is most likely to be positive emotion, at low levels of intensity, that presumably requires less effort than more intense emotional expression or negative emotion. Although positive emotions are about the attainment of a desired end state, negative emotions typically entail constructing a plan to either remove an obstacle to a goal, as in the case of anger, or construct a new goal when a desired end state is lost, as with sadness (see the discussion in Stein & Levine, 1987). Thus, the children are not likely to be saying words with either negative emotion, because of the extra cognitive cost negative emotion presumably requires, or with heightened emotional intensity, because of arousal effects.

The children's later transition to multiword speech (transition to sentences) when they were about 23 months old, on average, provided the opportunity to test the hypotheses of Effort and Engagement by extending the analysis of emotional expression around speech to the transition to phrases and simple sentences. The results of that analysis are presented in the first study below, the Transition to Sentences Study. The analyses of emotional expression around speech use all the events in the playroom regardless of what else the children and mothers were doing. However, the mothers and children were always acting and interacting, particularly as they played with the toys that were provided for them. Therefore, the second study, the Play Study, tested the Intentionality Model by examining the coordination of different kinds of expression in a subset of the children's behaviors, their actions with objects, to determine the relation between effort and engagement, and the tension between them, when the children were performing a well-defined motor task. Temporal patterns of expression (child speech, child emotional expression, and mother speech) were examined around episodes in play in which the children constructed thematic relations between objects, at the times of emergence and consolidation in word learning: first words and vocabulary spurt.

III. THE TRANSITION TO SENTENCES STUDY

Beginning to say phrases and simple sentences marks a transition in language development, as children learn syntax and move from saying one word at a time to combining words. The principles of relevance and elaboration, and the hypothesis of an essential tension between engagement and effort, provide conflicting expectations for the first study presented in this monograph: the analysis of emotional expression around speech at the transition to sentences. On the one hand, as we have just seen, children succeed in integrating the two systems of expression at the vocabulary spurt. This was demonstrated by higher levels of emotional expression around speech than predicted by baseline levels of emotional expression. We interpreted this finding at vocabulary spurt as evidence of engagement and the principle of relevance. The children were learning to talk about what they cared about, those things that were relevant to them because they were about the objects and circumstances of their feelings. We therefore expected continued evidence of engagement at the transition to sentences, with increased emotional expression above baseline levels in the context of speech. On the other hand, according to the principle of elaboration, children learn syntax for expressing more complex intentional states that cannot be expressed by saying only one word at a time. If more elaborate intentional states and learning syntax for their expression require effort, with an increased demand on cognitive resources, then emotional expression would decrease below baseline rates in the context of speech as an indication of such effort and the tension between engagement and effort at the transition to sentences.

Two further hypotheses are suggested by the hypothesis of effort. First, given the individual differences in age among the children at the times of developments in language, children who make the transition to sentences somewhat later may be learning syntax with more effort than children who are earlier learners. That is, some children may acquire language later or earlier than other children depending on the relative difficulty that individual children encounter in learning. We expected, therefore, that later learners would be less likely to coordinate the two systems of expression and would express less emotion in the context of speech than earlier learners, relative to their respective baselines, at the transition to sentences. Second, the discourse context can also influence the effort required for speech, depending on whether a child's speech includes part or all of what someone else has just said (imitated speech) or originates with the child (spontaneous speech). Speech that is spontaneous ought to require more effort than imitated speech, since spontaneous speech entails recalling words for expression without support from having just heard the words in the discourse. We expected, therefore, that children would express more emotion around speech when part or all of what they say imitated a prior model than when their speech was spontaneous.

RESULTS AND DISCUSSION

The frequencies, means, and standard deviations of *all* speech tokens, as well as only imitated speech and only spontaneous speech, at the time of transition to sentences are presented in Table 1 for the first half hour of observation in the playroom. (Only 11 children are included in this analysis because one of the children experienced severe family problems followed by a veritable plateau in language acquisition beyond the vocabulary spurt.) The baseline data for the lag sequential analyses are presented for the individual children in Table 2, and consist of the percentage baseline rates for emotional expression at the target speech intervals and the 1-s lag intervals throughout the observation. The target baseline rates are the percentage of emotional expression in all the frames of the first half hour; the lag baseline rates are the percentage of all the 1-s intervals in the first half hour in which emotional expression was observed. For example, the child Vivian, a girl (Vi,f), expressed emotion in 22.3% of all of the 1-s intervals, and in 19.7% of all the frames in the first half hour of the playroom session at transition to sentences. The children are listed

TABLE 1

The Frequency of All Child Speech, Only Spontaneous Speech, and Only Imitated Speech, at the Time of Transition to Sentences ($N = 11$)

	Total	Mean	SD
All speech (tokens)	2011	182.82	69.75
Spontaneous speech (tokens)	1874	170.36	68.09
Imitated speech (tokens)	137	12.45	10.94

42

TABLE 2

THE NUMBER OF SPEECH TARGET EVENTS AND INDIVIDUAL BASELINE RATES
FOR EMOTIONAL EXPRESSION AT THE TIME OF TRANSITION TO SENTENCES

Child	Total Speech Targets	Lag Interval Emotion Baselines (%)	Target Emotion Baselines (%)
Sh,f	213	8.5	5.7
Co,f	212	12.9	9.2
Vi,f	142	22.3	19.7
Cl,m	280	12.0	13.0
Di,f	97	6.8	5.0
Ha,m	93	13.4	13.2
Ch,m	222	7.9	5.5
Ro,m	207	13.0	10.2
Je,f	139	36.6	31.2
Gr,f	291	10.5	9.6
Al,m	115	36.2	29.6

Note.—The children are listed by the first two letters of their pseudonyms in order of age, from youngest to oldest, with gender indicated as "f" or "m." Lag baselines are the percentage of 1-s intervals in the observation in which emotional expression occurred; target baselines are the percentage of emotional expression in all frames of the half-hour observation.

in Table 2 in order of their chronological ages at the transition to sentences, beginning with the youngest child.

The tendency for the children to express emotion in the moments before, during, and after speech at the transition to sentences is shown in Figure 6 as mean deviations from baseline (z-scores). In contrast to the result at vocabulary spurt, all of the scores around speech were below baseline levels of emotional expression, indicating that the children were more likely to be expressing neutral affect around speech at the transition to sentences. The decrease in emotional expression, relative to baseline, provides evidence of the effort that the transition to sentences requires. The general contour of the pattern of emotional expression for the group of children is only slightly reminiscent of the patterns seen at first words and at vocabulary spurt.

In order to examine the data for individual differences, the lag sequential analyses were repeated for the two subgroups of children who made the transition to sentences earlier or later, given that the children differed in age. The group was divided into two subgroups of later ($n = 5$) and earlier ($n = 6$) learners, who were above and below the mean age, respectively, at the time of the transition to sentences. The time spent in emotional expression and speech is shown for the two subgroups of earlier and later learners, at all three of the developments in language in

43

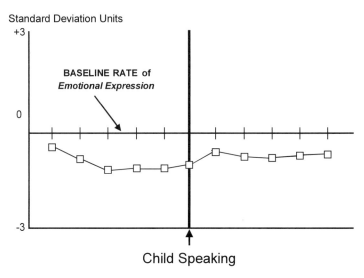

Standard Deviation Units

BASELINE RATE of
Emotional Expression

Child Speaking

FIGURE 6.—Temporal pattern of child emotional expression around speech at the transition to sentences (differences from baseline rates in standard deviation units).

Figure 7. Both earlier and later learners showed the same increase in time spent *speaking* (the percentage of video frames in each observation in which emotional expression was coded) from first words to vocabulary spurt to transition to sentences (similar to the result for the group of children as a whole in Figure 4). There were no differences between earlier and later learners in the percentage of time spent speaking at each of the language developments, even though they differed in age. Thus, level of language development rather than chronological age predicts amount of speaking time. In contrast, earlier and later learners did differ in the amount of time spent *expressing emotion*, with the later learners spending more time in emotional expression than the earlier learners. The differences between earlier and later learners in time spent expressing emotion were significant at first words, $F(1,10) = 5.046$, $p = .048$, and at vocabulary spurt, $F(1,10) = 9.687$, $p = .011$, but not at the transition to sentences, $F(1,9) = 2.790$, $p = .129$.

The intercorrelations for age of language developments and time spent in emotional expression are presented in Table 3. Time spent in emotional expression was also stable between the language developments: Time in emotion at first words was correlated with vocabulary spurt ($p = .008$) and with transition to sentences ($p = .029$), and time in emotion was correlated between vocabulary spurt and transition to sentences ($p = .003$). Age at first words predicted age at vocabulary spurt ($p = .032$) but not

44

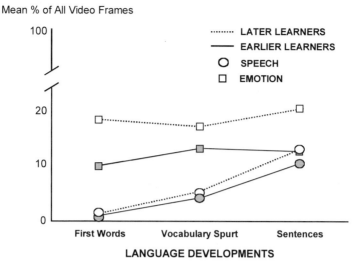

Mean % of All Video Frames

FIGURE 7.—Time spent speaking and expressing emotion shown as the mean percentage of all video frames (1 frame = 1/30th-s) in which each kind of expression occurred, later and earlier learners.

the transition to sentences (p = .063); age at vocabulary spurt was highly correlated with age at the transition to sentences (p < .001).

All correlations between age and time in emotional expression were positive: The more *time* children spent expressing emotion, the older they

TABLE 3

CORRELATIONS (PEARSON) BETWEEN AGE OF LANGUAGE DEVELOPMENTS
AND TIME IN EMOTIONAL EXPRESSION AT FIRST WORDS (FW),
VOCABULARY SPURT (VS), AND SENTENCES (S)

	Age, FW	Age, VS	Age, S	Emotion Time, FW	Emotion Time, VS
Age at FW					
Age at VS	.550*				
Age at S	.489	.923**			
Emotion time, FW	.610*	.659**	.696**		
Emotion time, VS	.487	.779**	.526*	.677**	
Emotion time, S	.213	.655*	.479	.585*	.773**

Note.—n = 12 at first words and vocabulary spurt; n = 11 at sentences.
*p < .05. **p < .01.

were at the time of developments in language. Children who expressed more emotion at first words were older at first words ($p = .018$) and at vocabulary spurt ($p = .01$), consistent with the earlier findings based on *frequency* of expression by Bloom and Capatides (1987b). The children who expressed more emotion at first words were also older at the transition to sentences ($p = .009$). Children who expressed more emotion at vocabulary spurt were older at both vocabulary spurt ($p = .001$) and at the transition to sentences ($p = .048$). Though time spent expressing emotion at first words and at vocabulary spurt predicted age of first words and vocabulary spurt, expressing emotion at the transition to sentences missed significance for predicting age at sentences ($p = .068$), possibly due to a decrease in statistical power with one less child in the group at the transition to sentences.

The tendency for the subgroups of earlier and later learners to express emotion around speech relative to their respective baselines is shown in Figure 8. In this analysis and in all the remaining analyses reported here, when different kinds of expression deviated from their respective baseline rates, the deviations clustered immediately around the target events. The 1-s intervals that showed an influence from the target varied somewhat in the different analyses. However, for the sake of consistency, statistical analyses of the data from the lag sequential analyses used only the

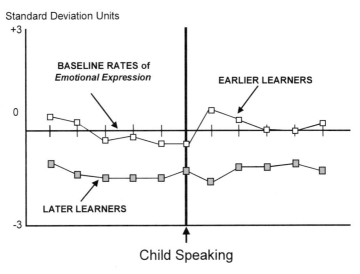

FIGURE 8.—Temporal patterns of child emotional expression around speech at the transition to sentences, later and earlier learners (differences from baseline rates in standard deviation units).

four intervals: the 1-s before target onset (T − 1), the duration of the target from onset to offset (T), and the first and second 1-s intervals after offset (T + 1 and T + 2). In both the Transition to Sentences Study and the Play Study that follows, in order to test the observed variance in deviations from baseline across the four intervals, z-scores were submitted to repeated measures analysis of variance, with time relative to the target (T − 1, T, T + 1, T + 2), expression type (child speech, child emotion, mother speech), and, in the Play Study, also language development (first words, vocabulary spurt), as within subject variables. For subgroup comparisons (e.g., between expression by earlier and later learners), mean deviations from baseline in the intervals were compared by paired samples *t*-test. Alpha level .05 was used for accepting results as reliable in all the analyses.

The temporal patterns of deviation from baseline over time shown in Figure 8 were not significant in a 4 (time: T − 1, T, T + 1, T + 2) by 2 (group: earlier and later learners) repeated measures analysis of variance, p = .321, but there was a significant effect of group, $F(1,9)$ = 12.301, p = .007. Earlier and later learners differed at $T + 1$, $t(4)$ = −10.567, $p < .001$, and at T + 2, $t(4)$ = −3.934, p = .017. Emotional expression was substantially below baseline levels for the later learners, even though the later learners were more likely to express emotion overall (with higher baseline rates) than were the earlier learners. The earlier learners, who were younger and also less likely to be expressing emotion overall, were more likely to express emotion around speech relative to baseline than were the later learners. Moreover, for the earlier learners, analysis of variance confirmed the temporal pattern of deviation from baseline, with an increase in emotional expression immediately after speech offset (in Figure 8), $F(1,5)$ = 1.640, p = .033.

The later learners, in spite of their overall tendency to be more emotionally expressive (with higher baseline rates for expressing emotion) than the earlier learners, were far less likely to express emotion around speech at the transition to sentences than predicted by their baseline levels. To the extent, then, that the decrease in emotion around speech indicated effort, speaking evidently recruited more cognitive resources at the transition to sentences for those children who made the transition later. The children who made the transition earlier were evidently acquiring language somewhat more easily. The transition to phrases and simple sentences required less effort for them, and they were better able to integrate the two forms of expression.

Finally, patterns of emotional expression around speech were expected to vary with the discourse context, with the hypothesis of effort predicting that emotional expression requires less effort in the context of imitated speech than in the context of spontaneous speech. The analysis

was repeated for speech that was imitated (i.e., child speech that repeated part or all of preceding mother speech) and speech that was spontaneous (without a prior model in mother speech). Child speech that
repeats all or part of a previous utterance ought to require less effort
than speech that entails recalling words for expression without such support from discourse. This hypothesis was tested by repeating the lag sequential analyses for speech that occurred spontaneously and speech that
imitated something of what someone else had just said.

The tendency to express emotion around imitated or spontaneous
speech relative to baseline is shown in Figure 9, and statistical analysis
confirmed the expectation that it was easier for the children to express
emotion around imitated speech, with a significant effect for discourse
(imitated, spontaneous), $F(1,9) = 7.756$, $p = .021$, and no effect of time.
The differences between the means of z-scores (deviations in emotional
expression around imitated or spontaneous speech) were very close to
the .05 level of confidence: T − 1, $t(10) = 2.203$, $p = .052$; T, $t(10) = 2.152$,
$p = .057$; T + 1, $t(10) = 2.188$, $p = .054$; and T + 2, $t(10) = 2.248$, $p = .048$.
Emotion was more likely to be expressed relative to baseline around speech
that occurred in imitation of what someone else had just said—that is,
speech that had a prior model in the discourse context. Thus, the results

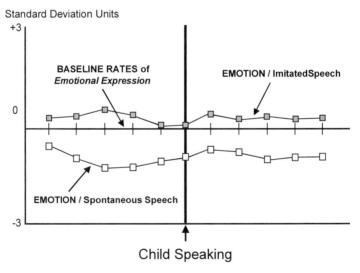

FIGURE 9.—Temporal patterns of child emotional expression around imitated and
spontaneous speech at the transition to sentences (differences from baseline rates in
standard deviation units).

in Figure 9 show coordination between effort and engagement for emotional expression and imitated speech, which hovered just above baseline, but emotional expression and spontaneous speech only showed the effort that was entailed.

SUMMARY AND CONCLUSIONS

The fluctuations in patterns of emotional expression around speech, at times of emergence and transition in language acquisition, show that the two systems of expression are not independent. Patterns of deviation from baseline show that emotional expression is clearly related to speech. As seen in the earlier study of vocabulary acquisition in the single-word period (Figure 5), the two systems are coordinated at both first words and at vocabulary spurt, although emotional expression at first words is below baseline in the moments of planning before saying words, and before increasing during and immediately after words. By the time of the vocabulary spurt, with achievement in word learning and a certain mastery in saying words, the pattern of coordination between the two systems is much stronger. Thus, the children are able to both express their emotions and, at the same time, tell others something of what their feelings are about. However, effects of effort are still discernible in the kinds of words (earlier learned, more frequent words) and the emotion (positive valence) that are expressed (Bloom & Beckwith, 1989).

The subsequent emergence of phrases and sentences is another transition in language acquisition, marking the beginning of grammar and learning procedures for sentences. Much stronger effects of effort are evident in the later emergence of phrases and simple sentences, with emotional expression substantially below baseline. These 1- to 2-year-old children were very good at expressing their feelings—readily and easily smiling, frowning, laughing, and crying over those things they cared about—and they had been since infancy. Nevertheless, the effort required for the transition to saying sentences interfered with their expressing emotion at the same time. However, effort has less effect on emotional expression when children have support from prior speech models (for imitating) in the discourse context. The increase in emotional expression during and immediately after words at vocabulary spurt had been interpreted as evidence of engagement, and led to the expectation of continued evidence of engagement in increased emotion while speaking at the transition to sentences. However, the effort of learning procedures for sentences and making the transition to sentences creates the tension between engagement and effort that is evident in the decrease in emotional speech around speech.

IV. THE PLAY STUDY

Earlier analyses of children's emotional expression around speech used all speech events, regardless of what else the children and their mothers were doing at the same time. In fact, however, the playroom afforded the children and their mothers many opportunities for different kinds of behaviors and actions with objects, and these actions and interactions were the context for their expressive behaviors. A key feature of the video-recorded observations in the playroom was the successive presentation of groups of toys introduced into the playroom according to a fixed schedule each month, beginning when the children were 9 months old. All the children were presented with the same groups of toys, in the same sequence, every month. The toys were balanced so as to provide equal time for play with manipulative and representational toys, and equal time for playing with toys from each of three traditionally gender-related categories (girl toys, boy toys, and neutral toys). Thus, the children's play with the toys in the playroom provided a carefully controlled opportunity to study the relations between action in play and child and mother expression, both in real time from moment to moment as activities unfolded in the playroom, and over developmental time in the second year. Because the children's object play was not coded at the time of transition to sentences, only analyses at first words and at vocabulary spurt can be reported here. (For description of the toys and how they were introduced into the playroom, see Bloom, 1993a, and Lifter and Bloom, 1989.)

ACTING WITH OBJECTS IN PLAY

Actions in play, emotional displays, and speech are alternative ways of expressing representations in intentional states. Children's words articulate the elements, roles, and relations between them in intentional states. The child might name the action or the objects or how they do or do not go

50

together. An emotional display is an expression of the child's appreciation for and feelings about a match or mismatch between what is represented in mind and the circumstances in the situation (Campos, Barrett, Lamb, Goldsmith, & Stenberg, 1983; Oatley & Johnson-Laird, 1987; Stein & Levine, 1987). The child might frown or cry if the goal of a construction in play is blocked, or smile when the activity is successful. Similarly, by acting with objects, children show us how they are thinking about the objects and what they know about them. When a child takes an object and puts it together with another object to construct a thematic relation between them (e.g., putting a bead in a cup or on a string), we can assume that the child had a representation of the configuration and a plan for acting represented in mind, and the child's action expressed the representation (Lifter & Bloom, 1997).

In the study reported here, child speech, child emotional expression, and mother speech were examined in the moments in play before, during, and after children put objects together to construct thematic relations between them. Studying constructions between objects in play capitalizes on the well-known tendency very young children have for appreciating that things go together to form the ordinary themes of everyday events. Young children's groupings of things are graphic and based either on geometric shape, or on "a relation of belonging drawn from the subject's past experience" (Inhelder & Piaget, 1964/1969, p. 45; see also Gelman & Baillargeon, 1983; Markman, 1989). Certain thematic relations between objects are afforded by their *physical* characteristics, consistent with groupings based primarily on shape, such as when one object can serve as a container or a surface to hold or support another object. Other relations, however, are also influenced by the *social and cultural experience* of everyday events, such as relations between a spoon and eating or between a truck and a roadway. These are thematic relations that are learned from custom and convention rather than being inherent only in the physical properties of the objects themselves.

Within the window of time in which a child takes one object, such as a spoon, and puts it together with another object, such as a cup, to create a thematic configuration between the objects, the child's action, speech, and emotion presumably express aspects of the same intentional states, and the speech the child hears is at least potentially interpretable by the child with respect to the child's intentional states. This window was operationally defined for this study to encompass the three phases of (a) planning, in the moments immediately before the onset of an act of constructing; (b) enactment, the time between the onset and offset of the construction; and (c) accomplishment (or abandonment), the moments immediately after the child succeeded in the construction (or abandoned the attempt if not successful). Thus, the temporal contingencies between

51

mother speech, child speech, and child emotional expression in the context of actions in object play were used as an index of the cognitive activity invested in the observed behaviors for testing the hypotheses of engagement and effort and the tension between them in development.

HYPOTHESES OF ENGAGEMENT AND EFFORT

The first hypothesis that guided the study of expressions around object play was the engagement hypothesis: Interest in the toys and in constructing the thematic relations afforded by the toys is expected to result in heightened arousal, with increased emotional expression and talk relative to the respective baseline levels of each around episodes of object play. However, the second hypothesis, the hypothesis of effort, conflicted with the expectations associated with engagement, suggesting the potential for tension between them. Under the assumptions of a general, single-resource model, with different behaviors depending on the same pool of resources, constructing relations between the toys in play, saying words, expressing emotion, and listening to mothers' speech in order to interpret it should all cost a child in cognitive effort. Therefore, saying words and expressing emotion are expected to diminish in general in the moments around constructing activity. Alternatively, competition between the two kinds of expression will result in a trade-off between them, with either words or emotional expression decreasing as one or the other increases. These demands on a child's cognitive resources are expected to be greatest at times of emergence and transition in language. However, the assumptions of a model of separate resources, with independence between different kinds of actions, leads to the expectation that expressive behaviors will not differ from baseline levels around episodes of object play as a result of effort.

Others have already shown that children tend neither to express such emotions as anger, joy, or sadness (Phillips & Sellito, 1990) nor to talk (Margulis & Anisfeld, 1991) at the same time they play with objects. However, the observed frequencies of speech or emotional expression were not compared to their probabilities of occurrence or expected frequencies in those studies. In no studies have both emotion expression and speech been examined in relation to each other or to other actions such as object play. Furthermore, mothers' speech has not been examined in relation to children's speech together with their emotional expressions and object play at the same time. However, we assumed that children attempt to interpret what they hear their mothers saying, and the effort of interpretation adds additional processing demands in the context of play.

SPECIFIC HYPOTHESES AND EXPECTATIONS

Developments we observed previously in the children's play (in Lifter & Bloom, 1989) allowed us to test, in the study reported here, the hypotheses of engagement and effort, and the tension between them, as well as other more specific expectations. The children's earliest action with the toys was to separate or take apart a configuration that either was given when the toys were presented originally or was subsequently constructed for them by their mothers. Toward the end of the first year the children began to put objects together to construct thematic relations, and for most of them achievement in constructions coincided with beginning to say words. Developments in the second year consisted of learning to construct different kinds of relations between the objects, and increases in both kind and frequency of different constructions were coextensive with an increase in words and the vocabulary spurt. The subcategories of object play are displayed in the tree diagram in Figure 10, which captures both their logical derivation and their empirical validity in the children's development.

In the period from emergence to achievement, in both object play and language, the children learned to construct relations between objects that were discrepant from the ways in which the toys were originally introduced into the playroom and more elaborated than simply putting one thing into or on top of another. For example, each time a set of miniature spoons, forks, and knives was introduced into the playroom,

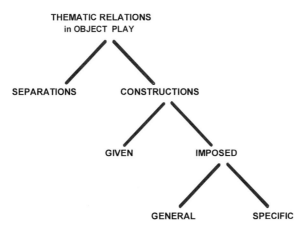

FIGURE 10.—Schematic representation of categories of object play and their development in the second year. (Adapted from Lifter & Bloom, 1989.)

they were collected together in a basket. Putting a toy spoon or fork back into the basket is a *given* construction because it recreates the original configuration, in contrast to an *imposed* construction such as putting the spoon in a cup or a doll's mouth, which creates a different relation between the objects. Given constructions depend on recalling the configuration between objects as they were originally presented; imposed constructions are discrepant from the original presentation of the objects and depend on recalling from memory other possibilities for relating two or more objects.

Imposed relations, in turn, are either general or specific. General constructions make use of those physical properties of objects that afford containment or support with no other thematic content (e.g., putting a fork into a truck or on top of a block). Specific constructions make use of more particular thematic content based on functional and conventional as well as physical properties of the objects in relation to each other, as when a child uses a toy spoon to feed the baby doll or puts beads on the string.

Emergence and achievement in object play were established on the basis of several converging criteria applied to the children's play activities in the playroom, as coded from the video-recorded observational data. Criteria for emergence of a subcategory of construction included at least five constructions of a type (e.g., specific thematic relations) that included at least two different constructions. The criteria for achievement doubled the criteria for emergence (i.e., at least 10 constructions of a type that included at least four different constructions). Given that play activities are expected to increase over time, and that earlier emerging behaviors are expected to continue as new behaviors appear and increase in frequency, a third criterion for achievement based on relative frequency also was used. Thus, achievement in a subcategory of thematic relations also required at least a 40% increase in the relative frequency of that category. (A 40% increase in relative frequency was used, because all the children showed an increase of at least 40% in each of the subcategories displayed in Figure 10, even though relative frequency in one or another category might have increased as much as 60% or 80% for some of the children; see Lifter & Bloom, 1989.)

The earliest imposed constructions were primarily general relations of simple containment or support. The major developments in the second year were a decrease in general constructions as specific constructions increased and became more frequent. Moreover, regardless of how old the children were at age of first words and vocabulary spurt, achievement in constructing imposed relations between objects was coextensive with first words, and achievement in constructing the more elaborated specific imposed relations was associated with vocabulary spurt. Thus, the primary development that occurred in object play between first words and vocabulary spurt was achievement in constructing imposed thematic relations that were specific to the functional and conventional properties of the objects (Lifter & Bloom, 1989).

In the present study of expressive behavior around object play, several conflicting hypotheses follow from the developments observed in both language and play in the second year. On the one hand, we assumed that specific constructions in play are more interesting to children and their mothers because (a) they are discrepant from the original configuration in which the toys were presented and, therefore, relatively novel, and (b) they represent achievement in learning at the vocabulary spurt. Thus, evidence of engagement is expected in a greater increase above baseline in emotional expression around specific constructions than around given constructions at vocabulary spurt (too few specific relations were constructed at first words for the lag sequential analyses). On the other hand, specific thematic relations constructed between the objects are also more elaborated by virtue of the functional and conventional knowledge they require, with more elements, roles, and relations between them. Therefore, under the assumptions of a general, single-resource model, constructing specific relations is expected to require more effort, with diminished emotional expression and speech relative to their respective baseline levels. Moreover, demands from several different kinds of behavior within the same window of time (object play, child speech and emotional expression, and interpreting mother speech) are expected to compete for the same pool of cognitive resources, with differences in the patterns of their variation from baseline levels relative to each other.

THE DATA FOR THE PLAY STUDY

Play activities depend on the representations a child is able to set up and hold in mind for expression by acting. As with coding emotional expression, we again opted for a more descriptive categorization scheme for coding object play in order to infer what a child has in mind about the objects and, therefore, knows about them at different points of time. Thus, while we controlled for the amount of time the toys were available for either manipulative or enactment play, these traditional interpretive categories were not used for coding play.

We looked at all the events in the playroom in which the infants constructed a relation between two or more objects. Together, the children produced a total of 981 constructions which served as the target behaviors for the lag sequential analyses of temporal contingency reported here. Given how frequently constructions occurred, we could assume that these actions represented what the infants did in their everyday activities and, therefore, what they knew about objects and their potential for thematic relations in everyday events. Certain relations were already given in the configurations in which the toys were introduced into the playroom; for example, wooden blocks were nested together and an array of peg figures already seated in a seesaw when the children first saw them each month. The children and their mothers took apart these configurations, put them back together in the same relation, or created different relations between the objects.

The procedures for coding object play and establishing reliability of coding were designed for the study reported in Lifter and Bloom (1989). All the computer entries for the object play coding decisions, together with the video records, were reviewed 3 to 5 years after the original study in order to verify the coding and establish times of onset and offset for the research reported here and by Wikstrom (1994). The criteria for coding onset time of the constructing activity were based on the assumption that a construction began when evidence of an intention to perform the action was first observed—for example, at the moment a child looked toward a second object after having picked up one object (e.g., Ruff & Lawson, 1990). Offset time of a construction was the moment the child either succeeded in completing the configuration or ended the construction activity after not succeeding. The average percentage agreement between independent coders was 92% for times of onset and 96% for times of offset. (The criteria and decision rules for deciding times of onset and offset for object play have been described by Wikstrom, 1994.)

Reliability of coding the features of the thematic relations in constructions was based on percentage agreement between independent coders. Coding by multiple judges for determining reliability was typically exhaustive or used several hundred coding decisions, and percentages of agreement after training were high—typically over 90% and never below 82%. In most instances, Cohen's Kappa (Cohen, 1960) was not appropriate for comparing percentage agreement with chance agreement because of the large number of coding fields—often as many as 7 decisions for each behavior (e.g., the objects used, the relation of mothers' actions to the construction, and so forth), which yielded too few data points in cells; see Howell (1992). Further description of the procedures and the results of reliability assessments can be found in earlier publications: in Bloom, Beckwith, and Capatides (1988) for the children's emotional expressions, in Bloom et al. (1993) for the children's speech, and in Lifter and Bloom (1989) and Wikstrom (1994) for object play. In sum, the results of four independent sets of procedures for transcribing child and mother speech and coding emotional expression and object play were recruited from previous studies for the purpose of the study reported here.

TABLE 4

THE FREQUENCY OF PLAY TARGET EVENTS (CONSTRUCTIONS),
CHILD AND MOTHER SPEECH TOKENS, AND CHILD EMOTIONAL EXPRESSIONS
AT FIRST WORDS ($n = 11$) AND VOCABULARY SPURT ($n = 12$)

	First Words			Vocabulary Spurt		
	Total	Mean	SD	Total	Mean	SD
Constructions	376	34.18	21.18	605	50.42	20.08
Child speech (tokens)	219	19.91	15.06	1,115	92.92	41.54
Mother speech (tokens)	3,549	322.64	140.22	4,691	390.92	159
Child emotional expressions	871	72.58	37.05	904	75.33	24.49

RESULTS AND DISCUSSION

The frequencies, means, and standard deviations of constructions and speech tokens are presented in Table 4 for both first words and vocabulary spurt. The baseline data for the lag sequential analyses are presented in Tables 5 and 6 for first words and for vocabulary spurt, respectively.

TABLE 5

THE NUMBER OF PLAY TARGET EVENTS AND INDIVIDUAL CHILD AND
MOTHER BASELINE RATES AT FIRST WORDS

		Baseline Rates (%)					
	Total Play Targets	Child Emotion		Child Speech		Mother Speech	
Child		Lag Interval	Target	Lag Interval	Target	Lag Interval	Target
Co,f	17	6.0	4.4	1.7	.6	24	10.8
Gr,f	30	18.1	15.2	.4	.5	31.7	15.3
Di,f	33	8.6	7.3	.9	.4	18.0	9.5
Ro,m	28	10.7	8.4	1.0	.4	42.0	26.8
Vi,f	31	17.5	14.0	1.2	.5	52.5	33.3
Al,m	11	23.0	19.2	.04	.05	32.4	15.0
Je,f	84	22.8	18.1	1.0	.5	21.0	10.6
Ha,m	64	6.7	5.4	.7	.3		
Cl,m	27	18.9	15.6	.6	.2	18.9	9.6
Re,m	23	19.4	15.1	.3	.1	8.0	4.0
Ch,m	28	23.8	18.2	1.6	3.0	49.6	28.1

Note.—The children are listed by the first two letters of their pseudonyms in order of age, from youngest to oldest, with gender indicated as "f" or "m." Lag baselines are the percentage of 1-s intervals in the observation in which speech occurred; target baselines are the percentage of speech in all frames of the half-hour observation. Mother speech data were not available for one child, Ha, at first words.

TABLE 6

		Baseline Rates (%)					
		Child Emotion		Child Speech		Mother Speech	
	Total Play	Lag		Lag		Lag	
Child	Targets	Interval	Target	Interval	Target	Interval	Target
Sh,f	78	7.5	5.8	11.7	4.6	60.7	35.0
Vi,f	40	13.6	11.2	6.2	3.1	49	27.6
Co,f	47	10.6	15.0	9.9	6.3	39.5	22.3
Cl,m	42	18.1	14.2	8.3	3.8	23.9	12.7
Di,f	71	10.5	10.1	4.3	1.9	23.4	13.4
Ha,m	78	14.4	11.2	6.6	3.1	47.3	28.7
Ro,m	19	10.4	7.7	7.1	2.7	40.9	19.9
Ch,m	76	17.9	14.1	11.7	5.1	47.4	27.5
Gr,f	43	14.8	11.2	14.8	7.7	55.8	32.8
Al,m	36	23.1	21.4	3.2	1.8	28.7	16.3
Re,m	32	23.5	19.9	8.3	4.3	6.8	3.3
Je,f	43	24.1	20.3	16.1	6.7	40.0	18.7

Note.—The children are listed by the first two letters of their pseudonyms in order of age, from youngest to oldest, with gender indicated as "f" or "m." Lag baselines are the percentage of 1-s intervals in the observation in which speech occurred; target baselines are the percentage of speech in all frames of the half-hour observation.

The information in the tables includes the number of target events (constructions) and percentage baseline rates for both targets and 1-s lag intervals for child emotional expression and child and mother speech. Percentages of child speech were quite low, particularly at first words, and the percentage of time the mothers were talking was relatively high, as can be seen from their respective baselines. For example, the child Je,f had a speech baseline rate of 1% for the 1-s lag intervals at first words, which means that speech occurred in 1% of all 1,800 1-s intervals in the first half hour of the observation session; her mother had a speech baseline of 21%, which means that she talked in about one fifth of all the 1-s intervals in the observations. The children are listed in each table in the order of their chronological ages at the times of first words and vocabulary spurt. One child, the youngest child to reach first words (at age 10 months), had no construction targets at first words, and mother speech data were not available at first words for a second child because of deterioration in the equipment. For these reasons, comparisons between child speech and emotional expression around play at first words and between first words and vocabulary spurt were based on 11 children, and comparisons of mother speech around play at first words were based on 10 children.

Child Speech and Emotional Expression, All Constructions

The patterns of differences from baseline in child speech and emotional expression before, during, and after constructions shown in Figure 11 were confirmed by a 4 (time: T − 1, T, T + 1, T + 2) by 2 (child expression: speech, emotion) by 2 (language level: first words, vocabulary spurt) repeated measures analysis of variance based on the 11 children for whom data were available at both first words and vocabulary spurt. The overall deviations from baseline for expression varied in the moments around the children's constructing activity from T − 1 to T + 2, depending on language development (first words or vocabulary spurt) and the form of expression (speech or emotion). The three-way interaction was significant, $F(3,30) = 6.61$, $p = .001$, with a significant interaction between language level and expression, $F(1,10) = 7.87$, $p = .019$.

The differences from baseline in child speech and emotional expression around constructions were tested separately at first words and vocabulary spurt, given the significant three-way interaction between expression, language level, and time. At first words, the interaction between expression and time was not significant. Speech hovered around baseline, emotional expression was 1 *SD* below baseline on average, and neither kind of expression changed in the moments around object play, with no effect

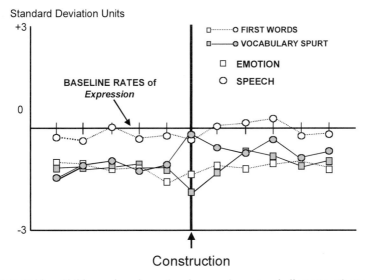

FIGURE 11.—Child speech and emotional expression around all constructions at first words and vocabulary spurt (differences from baseline rates in standard deviation units).

59

for time, $p > .05$. However, there was a significant effect for expression, $F(1,10) = 12.35$, $p = .006$, with the children more likely to say words than express emotion, $F(1,20) = 16.959$, $p = .001$.

A different picture emerged at vocabulary spurt. The interaction between expression and time at vocabulary spurt was significant, $F(3,30) = 6.34$, $p = .002$, with a significant effect for expression, $F(1,10) = 4.93$, $p = .05$. Speech increased during the constructing activity (T) and then decreased in the moments after with a significant effect for time, $F(3,30) = 7.639$, $p = .01$. The trend analysis revealed that the pattern was explained as a cubic curve from T – 1 through T + 2, $t(10) = 2.817$, $p = .018$, and attributable to the children being most likely to talk at T (although not more likely than predicted by baseline). However, emotional expression changed in the opposite direction—decreasing during play and then increasing immediately after—with a significant effect of time, $F(3,30) = 9.67$, $p < .001$. The trend analysis revealed that the pattern was explained as a quadratic curve in a direction opposite to that of speech, $t(10) = 4.833$, $p = .001$, and attributable to the decrease in emotional expression at T and subsequent increase from T to T + 2.

The general result in Figure 11 supports the hypothesis of effort: Emotional expression was below baseline levels, which means that the children were expressing neutral affect during and in the moments surrounding the episodes of object play. The tendency not to express emotion around object play at both first words and vocabulary spurt is consistent with what has already been reported in the literature by Phillips and Sellito (1990). The cognitive cost of attending to two objects, and recalling and then constructing a thematic relation between them, evidently competes with expressing emotion at first words and saying words and expressing emotion at vocabulary spurt. In the moments of planning, before constructing, emotion at first words and both speech and emotion at vocabulary spurt were, on average, about 1 *SD* below their respective baseline levels. In the moments of constructing, between onset and offset, speech increased and emotional expression decreased. This mirror-image between speech and emotion represents a trade-off between the two forms of expression and evidence of the need to distribute resources in connection with object play, providing further support for the hypothesis of effort. Moreover, this trade-off at vocabulary spurt between emotional expression and speech during object play contrasts sharply with the overall pattern of emotional expression around all speech at vocabulary spurt (Bloom & Beckwith, 1989, Figure 5 above): The two forms of expression were not integrated in the subset of activities that included constructing thematic relations between objects in play.

At vocabulary spurt, speech decreased immediately before the onset of play—evidently showing the effects of planning—and then increased to baseline during the time of the construction activity. The children were more likely to be talking at T than at T − 1, $t(10) = 3.55$, $p = .005$. However, and surprisingly, the children were more likely to be talking around object play at first words than at vocabulary spurt, and this difference between language level was significant, $F(1,10) = 6.16$, $p = .032$. At first words, speech hovered around baseline, and the children were more likely to say words than to express emotion relative to the respective baselines, even though emotional expression was relatively well developed and robust (Bloom, Beckwith, & Capatides, 1988), while speech was just emerging.

Thus, the effects of planning in the moments before constructions are not apparent from the results for speech at first words, and the question remains as to why speech did not also decrease around constructions at first words. The relative frequency of speech and constructions at the different language levels may have been a factor: Speech tokens were less frequent than constructions at first words but far more frequent than constructions at vocabulary spurt (Table 4), $X^2(1, N = 4) = 142$, $p < .001$. In contrast, emotional expressions were more frequent than constructions at both language levels. We can only speculate that speech incidents were too infrequent at first words to reveal an interaction.

In addition, children's earliest words have been described as indexical, "merely an accompaniment to an action in progress" before becoming symbolic (Piaget, 1962, p. 222), and "primarily associative" (Hollich et al., 2000, p. 86; also see Bloom, 1973, 1993a). Although words were only just emerging, constructions (primarily given relations and general relations of containment or support) had emerged earlier, in the pre-speech period (Lifter & Bloom, 1989). Thus, although constructions clearly entailed planning at first words, as shown in the decrease in emotional expression below baseline, early speech may not have differed from baseline because of the close associations between early words and the objects in constructions:

> [An early word is] not at first dissociable from the episode of its first encounter and enters into . . . a word-image representation in memory . . . [a] compound of utterance and episode [in] memory. . . . Because of their linked storage, recalling the word is interdependent with recalling other aspects of the episode. Thus, when some aspect of the same or similar episode reappears, these reencounters serve as perceptual cues for recalling the word/episode compound from memory. . . . Saying the word is dependent upon reencounters with the same or similar circumstances. . . . Later words are attached to more clearly defined concepts . . . abstracted out of those original episodes and the subsequent episodes in which the child continues to hear words. (Bloom, 1993a, pp. 83, 108)

61

Interpreting what their mothers were saying as the children played with the toys presented another demand on the children's attention and cognitive processing. Mothers were most often sitting with the children on the floor as they played with the toys and participated in the activity according to the child's demands and their own wishes (they were not given instructions to do anything with the toys). Analysis of the mothers' speech allows us to look at the convergence of the two forms of child expression with their mothers' speech to them, which presumably the children were attending to and interpreting at the same time as they played with the toys.

The patterns of temporal differences from baseline in mothers' speech and child speech and emotion around all constructions are shown in Figures 12a and 12b, for first words and vocabulary spurt, respectively. At first words, deviations from baseline were tested by a 4 (time: $T - 1$, T, $T + 1$, $T + 2$) by 3 (expression: mother speech, child speech, child emotion) repeated measures analysis of variance based on the 10 children for whom both play and mother speech data were available at both first words and vocabulary spurt. The interaction between expression and time was not significant ($p > .05$). The main effect for expression was significant, $F(2,18) = 6.64$, $p = .007$. The trend analyses revealed that the pattern was explained as a linear curve, $t(9) = 3.6971$, $p = .005$, attributable to the difference between mothers' speech and child emotional expression, $F(1,9) = 13.67$, $p = .005$, and the difference between child speech and emotional expression reported earlier.

Child and mother speech hovered around their respective baseline rates and did not differ except during the episode of constructing at T. Relative to their baseline rates of speech, mothers were least likely to be talking at T, in general, and significantly less likely to be talking at T than were their children, $t(9) = -1.93$, $p < .05$. This result echoed the earlier finding, in the study of conversational interaction by Bloom et al. (1996), that mothers and children tend not talk at the same time.

A different picture was evident at vocabulary spurt: The interaction between expression and time for the 11 children, shown in Figure 12b, was significant, $F(6,66) = 7.41$, $p < .001$, with main effects for both expression, $F(2,22) = 6.31$, $p = .007$, and time, $F(3,33) = 5.06$, $p = .005$. Relative to baseline, mothers were most likely to be talking immediately after the episode of play, less likely to be talking immediately before, and least likely to be talking at the same time as the children's constructing activity at T. When analysis of variance was repeated with only the 10 children for whom mothers' data were also available at first words, the interaction between expression and time continued to be significant, $F(6,60) = 5.87$,

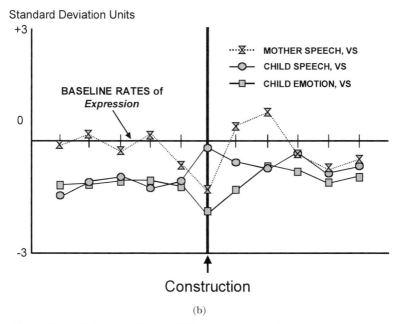

FIGURE 12.—Mother speech and child speech and emotional expression around all constructions at (a) first words and (b) vocabulary spurt (differences from baseline rates in standard deviation units). N = 10 children at first words and 11 children at vocabulary spurt.

$p < .001$, along with main effects for both expression, $F(2,20) = 9.59$, $p = .001$, and time, $F(3,30) = 5.72$, $p = .003$.

The interaction between mother speech and child speech at vocabulary spurt, in Figure 12b, was significant, $F(3,33) = 10.29$, $p < .001$, with a significant effect for time, $F(3,33) = 3.43$, $p = .028$. The trend analyses revealed that the pattern was explained as a quadratic curve, $t(11) = 2.3656$, $p = .04$, attributable to the patterns of mother and child speech deviating relative to their respective baseline rates in opposite directions during and after constructions. The children were more likely to be talking than their mothers at T, $t(11) = -2.66$, $p = .022$, and mothers were more likely to be talking than the children at T + 1, $t(11) = 1.79$, $p < .05$, and at T + 2, $t(11) = 2.85$, $p = .016$. The picture of responsiveness on the part of the mothers, to both children's play and speech, is consistent with the description by Tamis-LeMonda, Bornstein, and Baumwell (2001) of mothers' tendency to respond to play and speech.

The near mirror image between mother and child speech around constructions evident in Figures 12a and 12b shows the same turn-taking properties of conversations between children and their mothers, in general, that was reported by Bloom et al. (1996). The pattern of conversational turn-taking between them was well established by vocabulary spurt, and the mothers and children were not likely to be talking at the same time. However, the lag sequential analyses in the earlier study of conversation included all of the mother and child speech, and deviations from baseline were very strong. Both mother and child speech were each almost 3 *SD*s below their respective baseline rates during the target interval when the other was speaking. Most striking, mothers' speech was more than 4 *SD*s above baseline after the child speech target, and child speech was more than 4 *SD*s above baseline before the mother speech target.

The same pattern was observed with the subset of child-mother conversations around the children's constructing activity with the toys, but the amplitudes of the excursions from baseline were greatly diminished by comparison. Mothers continued to be responsive to their children's speech and to their play in the context of object constructions, but the increase above baseline in mothers speaking immediately after target play (and contingent child speech) was much less than was observed when all the child-mother conversations were examined regardless of activity. Thus, both the mothers and their children were talking to each other far less when playing with the toys than they were, in general, when all of their interactions in the playroom were included in the analysis.

The interaction between mothers' speech and child emotional expression at vocabulary spurt (Figure 12b) was not significant. However, the effect for expression was significant, $F(1,11) = 16.94$, $p = .002$, with the trend analyses revealing that the pattern was explained by a linear curve,

$t(11) = -4.1157$, $p = <.002$. The effect for time was also significant, $F(3,33) = 11.00$, $p < .001$, and the trend analyses revealed that the pattern was explained as a linear curve, $t(11) = 3.898$, $p = .004$. Thus, mother speech and child emotional expression showed the same pattern in the differences from their respective baseline rates around constructions, with the same trend from $T - 1$ to $T + 2$. Both child emotion and mothers' speech decreased when child speech increased at T, and both then increased when child speech decreased after T. However, the children were less likely to be expressing emotion relative to baseline, and mothers were more likely to be talking relative to their own baseline rate of speech, increasing above baseline at $T + 1$ and $T + 2$. The deviations from baseline in mothers' speech and child emotional expression differed at T, $t(11) = -3.05$, $p = .011$; at $T + 1$, $t(11) = -4.07$, $p = .002$; and at $T + 2$, $t(11) = -2.91$, $p = .014$.

In sum, results reported so far make clear that action in constructing thematic relations between objects influences expression by both children and mothers. The children's low incidence of emotional expression is particularly striking given the *overall* tendency for child emotional expression and child speech to occur together at vocabulary spurt, when other accompanying activity is not taken into account (Bloom & Beckwith, 1989, Figure 5 above). And the low incidence of both child and mother speech around the play activities relative to their baseline rates is also striking given the far greater excursions above baseline in both the children's speech *before* mother speech and mothers' speech *after* child speech that were observed in their conversations generally (by Bloom et al., 1996). Evidently, both children's emotional expression and conversational turn-taking occur primarily in other contexts, not when constructing thematic relations in object play

Expression Around Given and Specific Constructions at Vocabulary Spurt

The major conceptual development in play between first words and vocabulary spurt was achievement in constructing specific thematic relations. Consequently, *given* and *specific* thematic relations were the two subcategories of construction farthest removed in the developmental hierarchy (in Figure 10) and most different from each other conceptually.

Given constructions resulted when the children put the objects back together to re-create the configuration in which the toys were originally presented to them at each session in the playroom ($n = 241$, $M = 20.08$, $SD = 13.64$). Because the children had played with the same toys, and the toys were presented on the same schedule every month beginning at 9 months of age, these given relations had become familiar to the children and their mothers by the time of the vocabulary spurt. In contrast to given relations, the specific constructions ($n = 255$, $M = 21.25$, $SD = 13.30$)

were *discrepant* from the configurations in which the children saw the objects originally. Specific relations were also more *elaborated*, with more varied roles and relations between the objects than just the relations of containment or support (i.e., the general relations that resulted from putting one object inside of or on top of another object; see Figure 10).

The patterns of baseline deviation for child speech and emotional expression in the context of the given and specific constructions at vocabulary spurt are shown in Figure 13. The temporal deviations from baseline levels were tested by a 4 (time: T − 1, T, T + 1, T + 2) by 2 (child expression: speech, emotion) by 2 (play category: given, specific) repeated measures analysis of variance with all 12 children. The interaction between expression and play category was significant, $F(1,11) = 9.80$, $p = .01$, as was the interaction between expression and time, $F(3,33) = 4.71$, $p = .008$. The main effect of play category was significant, $F(1,11) = 8.03$, $p = .016$, and the effect of expression was also significant, $F(1,11) = 5.26$, $p = .043$. The effect of time did not reach significance, $F(3,33) = 2.38$, $p = .087$, which means that expression, in general, and the categories of play did not vary together from T − 1 to T + 2.

Considering just the *given* thematic relations, the interaction between expression and time was significant, $F(3,33) = 5.015$, $p = .026$, as was the effect for expression, $F(1,11) = 33.69$, $p < .001$, but the effect for time was not, $p > .10$. Thus, the difference shown in Figure 13 between child speech

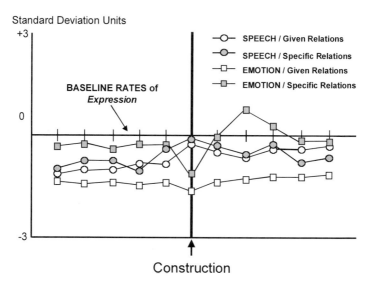

FIGURE 13.—Child speech and emotional expression around given and specific constructions at vocabulary spurt (differences from baseline rates in standard deviation units).

and emotional expression around given constructions was confirmed: The children were less likely to deviate from their respective baselines for speech than for expressing emotion (i.e., they were expressing neutral affect) at T, $t(11) = -5.14$, $p < .001$; T + 1, $t(11) = -4.03$, $p = .002$; and T + 2, $t(11) = -2.59$, $p = .025$.

Looking at just the constructions with *specific* relations, the interaction between expression and time was again significant, $F(3,33) = 3.36$, $p = .03$. The trend analysis revealed that the pattern was explained as a quadratic curve, with the children more likely to be speaking than expressing emotion relative to baseline and evidently not both speaking and expressing emotion at the same time. This trade-off between speech and emotion around both given and specific constructions again provides evidence for the effort hypothesis. The deviations from baseline for speech and emotional expression differed during constructing at T, $t(11) = -2.26$, $p = .045$, although the difference at T + 2 was not significant, $t(11) = 2.05$, $p = .065$ (by two-tailed test). Neither the main effect for expression, $p > .10$, nor the effect for time, $F(3,33) = 2.77$, $p = .057$, reached significance.

The statistically reliable interaction in Figure 13 between given and specific constructions was attributable to the patterns of deviation from baseline for emotional expression. The main effect on emotional expression of both play category, $F(1,11) = 10.55$, $p = .008$, and time, $F(3,33) = 6.73$, $p = .001$, were significant (the interaction between category and time just missed significance, $F(3,33) = 2.78$, $p = .056$). The children expressed far less emotion constructing given relations at vocabulary spurt compared with specific relations than would be expected from their baseline levels of emotional expression, and differences between the two kinds of constructions were significant at T − 1, $t(11) = -2.39$, $p = .036$; T + 1, $t(11) = -3.16$, $p = .009$; and TP + 2, $t(11) = -3.52$, $p = .005$ (by two-tailed test). In contrast, patterns of deviation from baseline for speech were not different for the two kinds of thematic relations.

The difference between the given and specific constructions in patterns of emotional expression provide support for the hypothesis of engagement in two ways. First, emotional expression around specific constructions was closer to baseline and, therefore, the children were more likely to be expressing emotion when constructing specific (new) than given (old) thematic relations between the objects. Second, and perhaps more important, emotional expression was below baseline at T in both subcategories, indicating that the children were expressing primarily neutral affect while constructing specific as well as given relations because of the effort that constructing activity required. A sharp increase in the slope of the curve followed the specific construction activity after T, as the tendency to express emotion increased and exceeded baseline when effort was no longer required. The pattern of emotional expression from T to T + 2 was tested by univariate repeated measures analysis of variance for time (T, T + 1, T + 2), and the result was significant, $F(2,22) = 8.06$, $p = .002$, with a significant linear trend, $t(11) = 3.219$, $p = .008$.

Evidence of engagement occurs when infants respond more with positive affect to relatively novel events than to events that are either already familiar or beyond their understanding (McCall & McGhee, 1977). Separating positive and negative emotional expressions in these analyses would have been informative but was not possible because negative expression was relatively infrequent, with too few data points. (Although large numbers of behaviors were included in the studies reported here, as seen in Table 4, increasingly finer subcategorization of behaviors resulted in too few data points for reliable lag sequential or statistical analyses, especially given the low level of statistical power with only 12 children in the analyses.) However, we do know that most of the emotional affect the children expressed in these play sessions was positive affect, both in general (Bloom, Beckwith, & Capatides 1988) and immediately after speech overall (Bloom & Beckwith, 1989). Therefore, we feel confident in comparing the burst in emotional expression immediately after constructing specific thematic relations to smiles of recognition following "mastery" and "concentrated attention" (e.g., McCall, 1972; Kagan, Lapidus, & Moore, 1978; Sroufe & Waters, 1976; Zelazo, 1972)—particularly because the increased emotional expression occurred immediately after the specific relations that represented achievement in learning at vocabulary spurt, but not after the given relations that were learned earlier, were much more familiar, and were evidently less engaging.

Mothers' Speech Around Given and Specific Construction at Vocabulary Spurt

Finally, on the assumption that the children were also attending to and interpreting what their mothers were saying to them, we looked at how the mothers' speech to their children varied around the given and specific constructions. The deviations from baseline rates of mothers' speech in the context of the given and specific thematic relations at vocabulary spurt are shown in Figures 14a and 14b, respectively. With data from only 10 children available at first words, subcategorizing object play yielded too few data points (with too few instances of specific constructions, in particular) for reliable analysis of mothers' speech.

The pattern of interaction shown in Figure 14a around the *given* thematic relations between mother speech and child speech and emotional expression was variable among the children. Only the effect of time was reliably confirmed by a 4 (time: T − 1, T, T + 1, T + 2) by 3 (expression: mother speech, child speech, child emotion) repeated measures analysis of variance, $F(3,33) = 3.080$, $p = .041$. When the two kinds of child expression

Standard Deviation Units

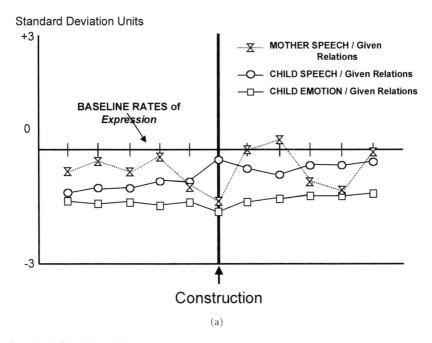

(a)

Standard Deviation Units

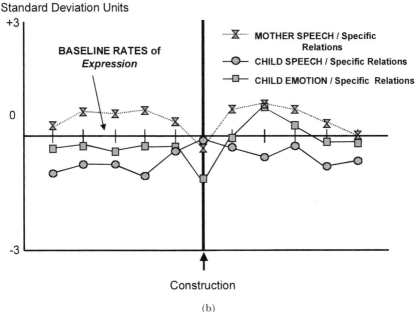

(b)

FIGURE 14.—Mothers' speech and child speech and emotional expression around constructions with (a) given thematic relations and (b) specific thematic relations at vocabulary spurt (differences from baseline rates in standard deviation units).

were tested separately for interaction with mother speech, the main effect of expression was significant for child emotional expression and mother speech, $F(1,11) = 7.982$, $p = .017$. Children deviated more from their baseline rates of emotional expression than their mothers deviated from their baseline rates for speech. The effect of time was significant for child speech and mother speech, $F(3,33) = 2.999$, $p = .045$, showing the same pattern of turn-taking with just the given relations as was observed for child and mother speech around all constructions (Figure 12b). Mothers' speech decreased when child speech increased at T, followed by an increase in mother speech above baseline in response to the children's constructing activity and contingent speech.

The pattern of interaction between mother speech and child expression around constructing *specific* thematic relations between objects, in Figure 14b, was not significant, $F(6,66) = 2.109$, $p = .064$. However both the effects of time, $F(3,33) = 3.332$, $p = .031$, and expression, $F(2,22) = 4.419$, $p = .024$, were significant. The effect of time was significant for child emotional expression and mother speech, $F(3,33) = 5.441$, $p = .004$, with both showing the same decrease at T followed by an increase above baseline at T + 1 and T + 2. However, the effect of expression did not differentiate between mother speech and child emotion, $F(1,11) = 3.816$, $p = .077$, meaning they covaried from T – 1 through T to T + 2 but did not differ from each other over time. In contrast, only the effect of expression was significant in the interaction between mother and child speech, $F(1,11) = 17.156$, $p = .002$, and the effect of time was not ($p > .10$), because mothers' speech decreased in relation to the increase in child speaking during the construction at T. Mother and child speech did not show the same pattern of turn-taking around specific constructions as around the given constructions at vocabulary spurt. Mothers were more likely to be speaking than their children both before and after the constructing activity.

The deviations from baseline in mothers' speech for the two subcategories of object play are reproduced in Figure 15. Mothers' speech around the specific and given constructions showed a main effect for time, $F(3,33) = 5.35$, $p = .004$, as indicated by the decrease at T and the increase after T. However, the main effect of play category was not significant, $F(1,11) = 3.88$, $p = .075$, although deviations from baseline around the given and specific constructions differed significantly during the interval of play (T), $t(11) = -2.69$, $p = .021$, and in the 1-s interval immediately before, $t(11) = -1.89$, $p = .05$. While their children were more emotionally expressive in the context of the specific relations, mothers evidently also found the richer, elaborated specific relations more interesting and talked more about them, in general, than about the familiar given relations. However, their tendency to respond, in general, to a child's efforts at construction at T + 1 and T + 2 evidently diminished the effect of play category.

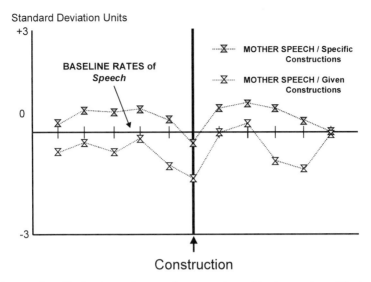

FIGURE 15.—Mothers' speech around constructions with given and specific thematic relations at vocabulary spurt (differences from baseline rates in standard deviation units).

SUMMARY AND CONCLUSIONS

Analyses of expression around children's object play produced four cumulative results. The first was that both forms of child expression— saying words and expressing emotion—were typically below their respective baseline levels around the children's constructing activities, and this general result provided support for the hypothesis of effort and a model of limited cognitive resources (Kahneman, 1973; van Geert, 1991). Planning and executing actions with the objects use cognitive resources that might otherwise be recruited for saying words and expressing emotion. Second, the children were more likely to say words than to express emotion around object play. Their speech, in general, hovered below or around baseline levels, with an increase to baseline during the actual time of constructing specific relations, in particular. This bounce to baseline during constructing was consistent with the assumption that words and actions both express elements of the same intentional state representations (Bloom, 1993a). Speech at baseline is also consistent with the principle of relevance. Children are inclined to talk about what they are doing or trying to do with objects. Moreover, the coextension of achievements in the more complex specific constructions (relative to general relations of just containment or support) along with the pattern of child speech around specific constructions at the vocabulary spurt provides support for the principle of elaboration.

71

The third result was the interaction between saying words and expressing emotion, with a trade-off between the two forms of expression. Emotional expression decreased when speech increased in the subset of the children's expressive behaviors around their constructing thematic constructions with objects. This interaction again suggests an increased demand on cognitive resources required by planning and constructing activity. This result is even more striking considering that in the earlier study of emotional expression around speech at vocabulary spurt, when all expressions were included in the analysis, speech and emotional expression were integrated and occurred together (in Figure 5 above, adapted from Bloom & Beckwith, 1989).

The fourth result was that patterns of mothers' speech reflected sensitivity to this cognitive activity going on in the minds of their children. Mothers were primarily *responsive* to the children's speech and actions with the toys. However, both the mothers and their children talked far less relative to their respective baseline rates in the subset of conversations around object play when compared to all their conversational interaction in the playroom session (as reported by Bloom et al., 1996). Mothers were least likely to be talking relative to baseline during the episode of construction, when child speech also increased, and most likely to be talking immediately after the construction as child speech decreased. Mothers also tended to talk more after the more elaborated specific constructions than other kinds of constructions, which complemented their children's tendency to express more emotion during the newly learned specific constructions.

V. GENERAL DISCUSSION

Actions depend on one's interest and engagement in an event as well as on the attention and effort they require. A balance is usually struck when we have to do two or more things either simultaneously or successively, and performance reflects accommodation to the effects of task difficulty. The research reported in this *Monograph* has only begun to tap the intricate and complex adjustments needed for the convergence of multiple behaviors in the stream of everyday activity—from moment to moment in immediate time, and over the course of the second year in developmental time.

The studies reported here are part of a larger program of research that explicitly set out to explore the connections between developments in three domains of ordinary activity—language, affect expression, and object play—in infants' development from age 9 months until age 2 years. The effects reported in the present study were of two kinds. Certain large, developmental effects extended across the period of language acquisition that began with the emergence of words, at about 1 year of age, and extended to the emergence of phrases and simple sentences about one year later, on average. Other effects were localized in the moment-to-moment, microgenetic contingencies of real time, as the children learned to say words and, eventually, sentences in the context of expressing emotion, playing with objects, and listening to (and presumably interpreting) what their mothers said to them.

Studies of language acquisition often take for granted that what children say in everyday activities or how children respond to an experimental manipulation provides straightforward evidence of what they know about language, as though language, as an object, is learned apart from other aspects of development and independently of other behaviors. However, the results of the research reported here show that children's actions and other expressions covary systematically, and the covariation among them is evidence that they influence each other and are not independent. Development leads to a variety of different abilities—in language, emotional expression, social interaction, and object play. However, another developmental task not ordinarily considered is the integration of these abilities in acts of expression and interpretation, in a seamless pattern of contingency in everyday events.

The behaviors we studied here were spontaneous rather than elicited, and naturally occurring rather than contrived, as infants and mothers interacted in a familiar playroom context. In contrast, behaviors in most studies are deliberate actions, elicited in response to stimuli in controlled experimental tasks. Though models of cognitive processing have been offered to explain experimental effects (e.g., Pashler, 1994), affect is rarely taken into account. However, affect and cognition are not separate. Research in the literature has shown both effects from affective arousal on cognitive processing (e.g., Kahneman, 1973) and the role of cognitive processing for affect and emotion (e.g., Mandler, 1984; Stein & Levine, 1987). These two complementary aspects of psychological process, cognition and affect, are entailed in effort and engagement. In the research reported in this *Monograph*, we interpret an increase relative to baseline in young children's emotional expression as evidence of arousal and engagement, and a decrease relative to baseline as the effect of cognitive processing and effort. The results of the study are patterns of temporal contingency in the distribution of behaviors over time. These patterns support an interpretation of complementary effects from both effort and engagement as a consequence the tension between them, and the necessity for a model of development that integrates them.

Developmental theory and research have always assumed, at least tacitly, a dynamic codependence among systems and subsystems, beginning at least with the organismic and contextualist world views of the giants of developmental theory: Piaget, Schneirla, Werner, and Vygotsky, as well more general psychological theorists such as Lehrman and Lewin. More recently, formal models of dynamic systems and development have been offered by, for example, Gottlieb (1991, 1997), Thelen and Smith (1994), and van Geert (1991). Nevertheless, sharply defined boundaries continue to exist between disciplines in psychology, and research and theory are generally pursued within rather than across discipline boundaries. Language, emotion, and cognition tend to be studied separately from each other, in large part because attempting to analyze collaborative influences on behavior introduces procedural, programmatic, and practical problems that are not easily solved (Bloom, 1993a, 1998). Nevertheless, the boundaries between traditional disciplines in psychology may be weakening because of the fundamental and systematic relations between them (Conner, 2001; Overton, 2002; Sternberg & Grigorenko, 2001).

The theoretical rationale for the research in this *Monograph* built upon three themes that led us to three conclusions. First, development depends on the child's intentionality as expressed by the child's actions, and, therefore, *performance counts.* Second, development depends on the essential tension between engagement and effort, with the result that *acquiring language is not easy.* And third, different domains of action are mutually dependent, because *language acquisition is integrated with other aspects of a child's development.* These conclusions that performance counts, that acquiring language isn't easy, and that language is acquired in the context of the rest of a child's development contradict several notions inherited from linguistic theory (since Chomsky, 1965): that competence, not performance, is what counts; that the illusory ease of acquisition must depend on innate linguistic representations to guide acquisition; and that language is a module, separate from the rest of human cognition, and dependent on domain specific (i.e., linguistic) processes. These ideas need to be drastically revised if not discarded altogether.

PERFORMANCE COUNTS

"The problem for the linguist, as well as the child learning the language, is to determine from the data of performance the underlying system of rules" of grammar (Chomsky, 1965, p. 4). This assertion precipitated the renaissance in language acquisition research that began more than 40 years ago. However, at the same time, the accompanying requirement that only "the study of performance models incorporating generative grammars" (i.e., formal, computational models of linguistic competence) may be "fruitful" (Chomsky, 1965, p. 15) led inevitably to denigration of the performance of language as it occurs in interpersonal and personal contexts. The disparagement of performance seriously constrained efforts to uncover either the processes whereby children acquire language in everyday events, or the processes whereby language develops over time.

One outcome of explanations of acquisition that depend on a formal, computational mechanism is the treatment of *language as an object* apart from and independent of other aspects of human behavior and learning. Further, the treatment of the *child as an object* is the outcome of research based only on specifically linguistic data (words, sentences, and sentence parts), independent of the children who acquire the language and who produce the data. However, the reality is that performance data of one kind or another in the interpersonal activities of daily living are what children have to work with: Language is learned in the performance of acts of expression and interpretation.

The research in this *Monograph* has to do with the process of acquisition in the context of children's actions. Performance counts because children learn the units of language in their efforts at interpreting what others do and say in order to attribute intentionality to them, and in the process of recalling words and sentence procedures for expressing their own intentionality. Learning does not happen in the moment in which a word or sentence exemplar is first encountered. That moment of first encounter provides only a fleeting, perhaps even ephemeral, exposure that can only begin the learning process. Children have to go beyond the first encounter, using forms in different circumstances, under different conditions, in order to own them as part of their linguistic knowledge. Children learn linguistic forms as the limits of their knowledge are stretched by new encounters that resist understanding or that cannot be expressed, much less articulated, by existing knowledge.

The research reported here joins the movement toward a more sub-jective, first-person perspective on children and their development (e.g., Bloom, 1993a, 1998, 2000a; Budwig, 1995; Lucariello, 1995; Zukow, 1990), and the growing body of research into the cognitive-social-pragmatic cir-cumstances of language learning (e.g., beginning with Anglin, 1977; Bates, 1976; Bloom, 1970, 1973; Nelson, 1974, and including, more recently, Baldwin, 1993; Bloom, 1991, 1993a; Hollich et al., 2000; Lucariello, 1987; Ninio & Snow, 1996; Tomasello, 1988). Children are learning far more about language than just formal linguistic units (sounds, words, and mor-phological and syntactic procedures); moreover, the linguistic units cannot be acquired and represented in the mind of the child apart from their cognitive-social-pragmatic entailments.

In sum, children learn the language in acts of interpretation. They strive to interpret the words and sentences that embody, make manifest, what others have in mind so as to set up a matching representation in their own minds for shared understanding. And children learn the lan-guage in acts of expression. They strive to access linguistic units they already know something about for articulating the words and sentences that can embody, make manifest, what they have in mind, so as to share contents of mind with other persons in new and different circumstances.

ACQUIRING LANGUAGE ISN'T EASY

The basic premise in formal linguistic theory is that language is a "distinct piece of the biological makeup of our brains ... a complex, specialized skill, which develops in the child spontaneously, without con-scious effort" (Pinker, 1994, p. 18). The results of the research reported here challenge that claim. Acquiring language, particularly in the initial transition to first words and the subsequent transition to phrases and simple sentences, takes work—it doesn't happen easily, much less auto-matically. The claims for innate linguistic representations (e.g., from

Chomsky, 1965, to Pinker, 1999) rest at least in part on the undocumented assumption that language acquisition is largely accomplished by 3 years of age. To be sure, most 3-year-old children have learned quite a few words and acquired much of what they need to know for sentences. But by no means does the 3-year-old have it all. Much more of the language is still to be acquired, and the development of language continues well into the school years. Moreover, the 3-year-old has been working at learning language virtually since birth—the very first associations with sound are already being formed in the womb (Fifer & Moon, 1995). In the ensuing first year of life, infants take apart the stream of speech they hear around them, bit by bit, tediously segmenting the pieces of the signal, and then begin, toward the end of the first year, to associate the pieces of sound with elements of meaning (e.g., Jusczyk, 1997, 1999).

Word learning begins slowly at the end of the first year, before picking up speed toward the end of the second year. The first phrases and simple sentences then begin hesitantly, and proceed gradually and tentatively to increase in length and complexity. In the Intentionality Model, the fundamental explanation for acquiring language is in the dialectical *tension* between engagement and effort. Engagement in the personal and physical world provides the motivation to express and articulate increasingly elaborate and discrepant representations. Effort is required to learn the language for expressing and interpreting these representations, particularly when cognitive resources need to be shared with other developments and actions that are contingent on language.

The transition to saying phrases and simple sentences is, itself, evidence of the increasing elaboration of intentional states. In object play, the specific thematic relations children construct, with different roles and relations between elements, are another example of more elaborate representations, compared to general relations of only containment and support. Specific constructions with objects are also discrepant compared to given constructions that reproduce the configurations in which the objects are originally encountered. In this study, children were evidently more engaged in constructing more elaborate specific relations, and less engaged in the more familiar given relations, as judged from the different patterns of emotional expression around each. Speech was below baseline levels for both kinds of constructions and only reached baseline during the actual interval between times of onset and offset of the constructing activity. The decrease below baseline in speaking in the context of both specific and given constructions reflects the effort that speech entails in the context of constructing activity.

The dialectical tension between engagement and effort originates in discrepancy, for example between what a child and other persons have in mind, and the child's mental plan and existing events in the context.

77

Tension also results from discrepancy between what the child already knows about the language and representations in mind that require new linguistic knowledge for expression. This tension is evident when comparing the interaction between speech and emotional expression at the transition to sentences, a time of emergence (in the study reported here), to their interaction at vocabulary spurt, a time of achievement and consolidation (in the study reported by Bloom and Beckwith, 1989). Tension is also evident in the interaction between the different kinds of expressions in the context of the different thematic relations the children constructed between the objects at first words and vocabulary spurt.

The general decrease in expressive behaviors below their baseline levels, particularly at times of transition, and the systematic covariation between expressive behaviors were evidence of the competition for scarce resources expected in a single resource model. "Dual-task costs should occur only to the extent that two tasks tap into the same resources" (Guttentag, 1989, p. 155). The results of these studies provide evidence of competing demands on the same pool of resources for different behaviors and support for a single resource model. The resources needed to construct intentional state representations and express them are most probably not drawn from separate resource pools for affect, to support emotional expression; cognition, to support object constructions, speech, and interpreting the speech of others; and movement, to support actions of expression and constructing. A model of independence between these different behaviors and their development is neither intuitively likely nor supported empirically. Instead, resources are shared among efforts at language and the cognitive activity required for constructing relations between objects in play, expressing emotion, and listening and interpreting to mothers' speech. Make no mistake about it, acquiring language requires *effort*; children work at it; and all aspects of the child's development—cognitive, social, affective, and linguistic—contribute to the acquisition process.

LANGUAGE IS ACQUIRED IN THE CONTEXT OF THE REST OF A CHILD'S DEVELOPMENT

The connections between language acquisition and other aspects of development are seen in the mutual influence among different actions. The results of an earlier study had documented the convergence of emotional expression and speech at vocabulary spurt, and this result was interpreted as evidence that the children had succeeded in integrating the two forms of expression (Bloom & Beckwith, 1989). However, at the time of emergence and transition to phrases and simple sentences, the integration of speech and emotional expression broke down. Even though the children continued to express emotion in general in these sessions and at the same rate as they had earlier at first words and vocabulary spurt, they were no longer expressing emotion in the moments around speaking at the time of transition to sentences. We have no reason to doubt that they were still motivated to talk about the objects of engagement and their attitudes toward them, things that were relevant. Nevertheless, the effort of using their emerging knowledge of procedures for sentences evidently preempted expressing emotion at the same time.

Furthermore, play actions that expressed a mental plan to create a thematic relation between objects evidently interfered with both forms of expression. Just as saying words and sentences can resolve the discrepancy between what the child and other persons have in mind, the child's constructing activity is another instance of resolving discrepancy: The child has a plan in mind, and that plan includes a configuration with a thematic relation between objects that are, so far, separate entities. The act of constructing the configuration resolves the discrepancy. Children are more likely to talk than to express emotion during the interval of constructing activity (between times of onset and offset), and more likely to express emotion than to talk immediately after the constructing activity, but both forms of expression are less than expected from their baseline levels.

The main effect of emotion and the interaction between speech and emotion around object play were statistically significant in the research reported here, but none of the main effects for speech in relation to the subcategories of play was reliable. The lack of statistical reliability for speech relative to baseline around object play may be attributable to variation among the children in their patterns of temporal contingency when constructing specific relations, in particular. Specific constructions included both inanimate objects (pushing the truck on a roadway) and animate surrogates (feeding the doll with a spoon). More speech was observed in connection with the animate surrogate toys than inanimate specific toys (from our general observations of the video tapes). Only some of the children progressed to creating specific constructions with the animate surrogate toys (Lifter & Bloom, 1989), which may have contributed to the variation among the children in the temporal patterns of speech around specific constructions. Otherwise, the differences among the children were unrelated to what else we know about them, such as chronological age, number and frequency of words, or differences among them in gender, race, or ethnicity.

The mutual effects among different behaviors are further illuminated by mothers' speech, which children are presumably interpreting, in relation to child actions and expressions. From our earlier research, we know that children are most likely to be talking immediately before mothers' speech; mothers are most likely to say something immediately after their children say something; and both mother and child are least likely to be talking at the same time, both at first words and at vocabulary spurt (Bloom et al., 1996). In the present study, with object play as the target event, the children were most likely to be talking during the constructing activity; their mothers were least likely to be talking to them at the same time during the construction. Mothers' speech was most likely to occur immediately after both child speech and constructing activity. Mothers' tendency to respond to the children's object play with the toys, therefore, could not be disentangled from their responsiveness to the children's speech in conversation; they evidently were responsive to both (see Tamis-LeMonda et al., 2001).

Thus, the results reported here confirm that mothers are primarily *responsive* rather than directive in the context of children's play with objects as well as in their conversational interactions. Nevertheless, both the mothers and children talked substantially less relative to their respective baseline rates when the children were constructing relations between objects in play than they talked in general in all of their conversations regardless of activity in the playroom. Deviations from baselines were as great as 4 *SDs*, on average, in the pattern of mother-child turn-taking at vocabulary spurt (Bloom et al., 1996). An interesting question for future research is just what the mothers and children were doing most of the time they were talking to each other in the playroom. The relatively low levels of both speech and emotional expression in the context of object play is consistent with results reported for emotional expression by Phillips and Sellito (1990) and for speech by Margulis and Anisfeld (1991). In addition, however, the study reported here revealed differential effects from the different kinds of thematic relations the children constructed between objects, as well as the interaction between speech and emotion during object play.

The variation in expressions around the different subcategories of thematic relations provides independent validation of the subcategories and their developmental hierarchy reported in Lifter and Bloom (1989) (see Figure 10). The different subcategories of constructions were identified originally on the basis of the sequence in which they appeared in the children's spontaneous play in the second year. In the present study, differences in the patterns of temporal contingency between speech and emotional expression in the context of given and specific constructions confirm the psychological reality of these subcategories for the children. Furthermore, the increase in emotional expression relative to baseline immediately after the *specific* thematic constructions, compared with given constructions, is evidence in support of the hypothesis of engagement for development more generally. The children were most likely to express

emotion immediately after constructing the specific relations that represented achievement in learning for them at vocabulary spurt.

Several other studies suggest how different behaviors may influence
each other early in their development in the second year. For example,
the coordination of gaze direction with speech, emotional expression, and
play with toys increases and develops over time (Schieffelin, 1983). In
addition, gesture and speech are not coordinated initially, and semantic
coherence, temporal synchrony, and integration between them develop
into a single system of communication only with development (Butcher &
Goldin-Meadow, 2000). Thus, both relative task demands and developments over time contribute to the distribution of resources for the convergence and integration of different aspects of behavior.

In sum, during the period in which we studied them, the children acquired a basic vocabulary and began to acquire the procedures for phrases
and simple sentences. At the same time, we can assume that they were also
learning to participate in increasingly elaborated interactions with persons as well as objects, and to regulate their emotional displays according
to increasing personal and social demands in the everyday events of their
lives. A critical aspect of these developments is the necessary adjustments
in timing and coordination required between different behaviors according to the extent of effort and relative engagement invested in them.

CONCLUSIONS

Many things inform what we do, including prior experiences in memory, the actions of other persons, and chance encounters of one or another kind. Both endogenous and exogenous influences are mediated by
our intentional states: the representations in consciousness that result from
perceptions and actions. These representations are not, themselves, available for study. Instead we can only look to the actions that are their
expression, which in this study were the children's play, speech, and emotional expressions and the speech of their mothers to them in the moments around constructions in object play. We assume that aspects of the
same intentional state representations are made manifest by the different
actions and expressions occurring within the same window of time. Speaking, interpreting what is said by other persons, expressing emotion, and
constructing thematic relations between objects all embody—are expressions of—aspects of the same underlying intentional states. The child's
intentionality, therefore, provides the connecting links between the behaviors and the processes underlying their coordination.

Language no doubt contributes to the pattern of language acquisition (what is learned and in what sequence), but it is not the cause of

acquisition. Other persons contribute to the motivation for learning (the need to share contents of mind that are discrepant) and provide input for learning, but other persons and interactions with other persons do not cause the learning. The brain provides the enabling and recording mechanism (the mechanisms for physical movement and how what is learned is inscribed in bodily tissue for continued accessibility), but bodily tissue is not the agent of anything. And the representations in intentional states do not cause or trigger actions. What, then, is the cause of development, in general, and language acquisition, in particular? The answer, in the Intentionality Model, is *the child*. It is the child who is the author of the mental representation in intentional states—taking what is presented to perception, apprehending it in terms of existing knowledge, and constructing intentional states with content about persons, objects, and events. The child sets up the representation in mind, adjusts it, and acts to express it. It is by virtue of being the agent of these mental processes in the construction of contents of mind, and the agent of their expression and interpretation, that the child, then, causes language development.

REFERENCES

Adamson, L., & Bakeman, R. (1982). Affectivity and reference: Concepts, methods, and techniques in the study of 6- to 18-month old infants. In T. Field & A. Fogel (Eds.), *Emotion and early interaction* (pp. 213–236). Hillsdale, NJ: Erlbaum.

Anglin, J. (1977). *Word, object, and conceptual development.* New York: Norton.

Archer, M. (2000). *Being human: The problem of agency.* Cambridge, UK: Cambridge University Press.

Arnold, M. (1960). *Emotion and personality: Psychological aspects* (Vol. 1). New York: Columbia University Press.

Baldwin, D. (1993). Infants' ability to consult the speaker for clues to word meaning. *Journal of Child Language,* **20**, 395–418.

Bates, E. (1976). *Language in context.* New York: Academic Press.

Beckwith, R., Bloom, L., Albury, D., Raqib, A., & Booth, R. (1985). Technology and methodology. *Transcript Analysis,* **2**, 72–75.

Bidell, T. (1988). Vygotsky, Piaget, and the dialectic of development. *Human Development,* **31**, 329–348.

Bjorklund, D., & Harnishfeger, K. (1990). The resources construct in cognitive development: Diverse sources of evidence and a theory of inefficient inhibition. *Developmental Review,* **10**, 48–71.

Bloom, L. (1970). *Language development: Form and function in emerging grammars.* Cambridge MA: The MIT Press. (Original doctoral dissertation, Teachers College, Columbia University, 1968).

Bloom, L. (1973). *One word at a time: The use of single-word utterances before syntax.* The Hague: Mouton.

Bloom, L. (1991). *Language development from two to three.* Cambridge: Cambridge University Press.

Bloom, L. (1993a). *The transition from infancy to language: Acquiring the power of expression.* Cambridge: Cambridge University Press.

Bloom, L. (1993b). Transcription and coding for child language research: The parts are greater than the whole. In J. Edwards & M. Lampert (Eds.), *Transcription and coding methods for language research* (pp. 149–166). Hillsdale, NJ: Erlbaum.

Bloom, L. (1994). Meaning and expression. In W. Overton & D. Palermo (Eds.), *The ontogenesis of meaning* (pp. 215–235). Hillsdale, NJ: Erlbaum.

Bloom, L. (1998). Language acquisition in its developmental context. In W. Damon (Series Ed.) & D. Kuhn & R. Siegler (Vol. Eds.), *Handbook of child psychology: Vol. II. Cognition, perception, and language* (pp. 309–370). New York: Wiley.

Bloom, L. (2000a). The intentionality model of word learning: How to learn a word, any word. In R. Golinkoff, K. Hirsh-Pasek, L. Bloom. L. Smith, A. Woodward, N. Akhtar,

M. Tomasello, & G. Hollich, *Becoming a word learner: A debate on lexical acquisition* (pp. 19–50). New York: Oxford University Press.

Bloom, L. (2000b). Intentionality and theories of intentionality in development. *Human Development,* **43,** 178–185.

Bloom, L. (2000c). Pushing the limits on theories of word learning. Commentary on Hollich, G., Hirsh-Pasek, K., & Golinkoff, R., Breaking the language barrier: An emergentist coalition model for the origins of word learning. *Monographs of the Society for Research in Child Development,* **65** (3, Serial No. 262, 124–135).

Bloom, L. (2001). Language acquisition and the child: Developmental and Theoretical Tensions. Keynote Address. In A. Do, L. Domínguez, & A. Johansen (Eds.), *BUCLD 25: Proceedings of the 25th annual Boston University Conference on Language Development* (pp. 16–33). Medford, MA: Cascadilla Press.

Bloom, L., & Beckwith, R. (1989). Talking with feeling: Integrating affective and linguistic expression in early language development. *Cognition and emotion,* **3,** 313–342.

Bloom, L., Beckwith, R., & Capatides, J. (1988). Developments in the expression of affect. *Infant Behavior and Development,* **11,** 169–186.

Bloom, L., Beckwith, R., Capatides, J., & Hafitz, J. (1988). Expression through affect and words in the transition from infancy to language. In P. Baltes, D. Featherman, & R. Lerner (Eds.), *Life-span development and behavior* (Vol. 8, pp. 99–127). Hillsdale, NJ: Erlbaum.

Bloom, L., & Capatides, J. (1987a). Sources of meaning in complex syntax: The sample case of causality. *Journal of Experimental Child Psychology,* **43,** 112–128.

Bloom, L., & Capatides, J. (1987b). Expression of affect and the emergence of language. *Child Development,* **58,** 1513–1522.

Bloom, L., & Lahey, M. (1978). *Language development and language disorders.* New York: Wiley.

Bloom, L., Margulis, C., Tinker, E., & Fujita, N. (1996). Early conversations and word learning: Contributions from child and adult. *Child Development,* **67,** 3154–3175.

Bloom, L., Rocissano, L., & Hood, L. (1976). Adult-child discourse: Developmental interaction between information processing and linguistic knowledge. *Cognitive Psychology,* **8,** 521–552.

Bloom, L., Tinker, E., & Margulis, C. (1993) The words children learn: Evidence against a noun bias in early vocabularies. *Cognitive Development,* **8,** 431–450.

Bratman, M. (1987). *Intention, plans, and practical reason.* Cambridge, MA: Harvard University Press.

Brentano, F. (1966) *The true and the evident.* English edition edited by R. Chrisholm, trans. by R. Chrisholm, I. Politzer, & K. Fischer. New York: Humanities Press. Originally published in 1930, Leipzig: Felix Meiner.

Bruner, J. (1981). Intention in the structure of action and interaction. In L. Lipsett (Ed.), *Advances in infancy research* (Vol. 1, pp. 41–56). Norwood, NJ: Ablex.

Bruner, J. (1983a). *Child's talk, Learning to use language.* New York: W.W. Norton.

Bruner, J. (1983b). The acquisition of pragmatic commitments. In R. Golinkoff (Ed.), *The transition from prelinguistic to linguistic communication* (pp. 27–42). Hillsdale, NJ: Erlbaum.

Budwig, N. (1995). *A developmental-functionalist approach to child language.* Mahwah, NJ: Erlbaum.

Butcher, C., & Goldin-Meadow, S. (2000). Gesture and the transition from one- to two-word speech: When hand and mouth come together. In D. McNeill (Ed.), *Language and gesture* (pp. 235–257). New York: Cambridge University Press.

Campbell, R. (1979). Cognitive development and child language. In P. Fletcher & M. Garman (Eds.), *Language acquisition* (2nd ed., pp. 419–436). Cambridge: Cambridge University Press.

Campbell, R. (1986). Language acquisition and cognition. In P. Fletcher & M. Garman (Eds.), *Language acquisition: Studies in first language development* (2nd ed., pp. 30–48). Cambridge, Cambridge University Press.

Campos, J., Barrett, K., Lamb, M., Goldsmith, H., & Stenberg, C. (1983). Socioemotional development. In P. Mussen (Series Ed.) & M. Haith & J. Campos (Vol. Eds.), *Handbook of child psychology: Vol. 2. Infancy and developmental psychobiology* (pp. 783–915). New York: Wiley.

Capatides, J. (1990). *Mothers' socialization of their children's experience and expression of emotion.* Unpublished doctoral dissertation, Teachers College, Columbia University.

Capatides, J., & Bloom, L. (1993). Underlying process in the socialization of emotion. In C. Rovee-Collier (Ed.), *Advances in infancy research* (Vol. 8, pp. 99–138). Hillsdale, NJ: Erlbaum.

Chandler, M. J., & Sokol, B. (in press). *Level this, level that: The place of culture in the construction of the self.* In C. Raeff & J. B. Benson (Eds.), *Culture and development: Essays in honor of Ina Uzgiris.* New York: Routledge.

Chomsky, N. (1959). Review of B. F. Skinner, Verbal behavior. *Language*, **35**, 26–58.

Chomsky, N. (1965). *Aspects of the theory of syntax.* Cambridge, MA: MIT Press.

Cohen, J. (1960). A coefficient of agreement for nominal scales. *Educational and Psychological Measurement*, **20**, 37–46.

Connell, J., & Furman, W. (1984). The study of transitions: Conceptual and methodological issues. In R. Emde & R. Harmon (Eds.), *Continuities and discontinuities in development* (pp. 153–173). New York: Plenum.

Conner, A. (2001). They all answer to 'psychologist.' *APS Observer*, **14**, 1ff.

Danto, A. (1973). *Analytical philosophy of action.* Cambridge: Cambridge University Press.

Danto, A. (1983). Toward a retentive materialism. In L. Cauman, I. Levi, C. Parsons, & R. Schwartz (Eds.), *How many questions? Essays in honor of Sidney Morgenbesser* (pp. 243–255). Indianapolis: Hackett.

Dennett, D. (1978). *Brainstorms.* Montgomery, VT: Bradford Books.

Dreyfus, H. (Ed.) (1982). *Husserl, intentionality, and cognitive science.* Cambridge MA: The MIT Press.

Easterbrook, J. (1959). The effect of emotion on cue utilization and the organization of behavior. *Psychological Review*, **66**, 183–201.

Ekman, P., & Friesen, W. (1978). *Facial Action Coding System.* Palo Alto, CA: Consulting Psychologists.

Emde, R. (1984). Levels of meaning for infant emotions: A biosocial view. In K. Scherer & P. Ekman (Eds.), *Approaches to emotion* (pp. 77–107). Hillsdale, NJ: Erlbaum.

Emde, R., & Harmon, R. (1984). Entering a new era in the search for developmental continuities. In R. Emde & R. Harmon (Eds.), *Continuities and discontinuities in development* (pp. 1–11). New York: Plenum.

Fantz, R. (1964). Visual experience in infants: Decreased attention to familiar patterns relative to novel ones. *Science*, **146**, 668–670.

Fauconnier, G. (1985). *Mental spaces: Aspects of meaning construction in natural language.* Cambridge, MA: MIT Press.

Fifer, W., and Moon, C. (1995). The effects of fetal experience with sound. In J. Lecanuet, W. Fifer, N. Krasnegor, & W. Smotherman (Eds.), *Fetal behavior: A psychobiological perspective* (pp. 351–366). Hillsdale, NJ: Erlbaum.

Freud, S. (1962). Infantile sexuality. In S. Freud, *Three essays on the theory of sexuality* (pp. 39–45). New York: Basic Books.

Gelman, R., & Baillargeon, R. (1983). A review of some Piagetian concepts. In P. H. Mussen (Series Ed.) & J. Flavell & E. Markman (Vol. Eds.), *Handbook of child psychology: Vol. 3. Cognitive development* (pp. 167–230). New York: Wiley.

Gelman, R., & Williams, E. (1998). Enabling constraints for cognitive development and learning: Domain specificity and epigenesis. In W. Damon (Series Ed.) & D. Kuhn & R. Siegler (Vol. Eds.), *Handbook of child psychology: Vol. II. Cognition, perception, and language* (pp. 575–630). New York: Wiley.

Gibbs, R. (2001). Intentions as emergent properties of social interactions. In B. Malle, L. Moses, & D. Baldwin (Eds.), *Intentions and intentionality: Foundations of social cognition.* Cambridge, MA: MIT Press.

Goldfield, B., & Reznick, J. (1990). Early lexical acquisition: Rate, content, and the vocabulary spurt. *Journal of Child Language,* **17,** 171–183.

Golinkoff, R. (1986). 'I beg your pardon?': The preverbal negotiation of failed messages. *Journal of Child Language,* **13,** 455–476.

Golinkoff, R., Hirsh-Pasek, K., Bailey, L., & Wenger, N. (1992). Young children and adults use lexical principles to learn new nouns. *Developmental Psychology,* **28,** 99–108.

Gottlieb, G. (1991). *Individual development and evolution: The genesis of novel behavior.* Oxford: Oxford University Press.

Gottlieb, G. (1997). *Synthesizing nature-nurture: Prenatal roots of instinctive behavior.* Mahwah, NJ: Erlbaum.

Guttentag, R. (1989). Age differences in dual-task performance: Procedures, assumptions, and results. *Developmental Review,* **9,** 146–170.

Harris, M. (1992). *Language experience and early language development: From input to uptake.* Hove, NJ: Erlbaum.

Hirsh-Pasek, K., & Golinkoff, R. (1996). *The origins of grammar: Evidence from early language comprehension.* Cambridge, MA, MIT.

Hoff, E., & Naigles, L. (2002). How children use input to acquire a lexicon. *Child Development,* **73,** in press.

Hollich, G., Hirsh-Pasek, K., & Golinkoff, R. (2000). Breaking the language barrier: An emergentist coalition model for the origins of word learning. *Monographs of the Society for Research in Child Development,* **65** (3, Serial No. 262).

Howe, C. (1981). *Acquiring language in a conversational context.* London: Academic Press.

Howell, D. (1992). *Statistical methods for psychology* (3rd ed). Boston: Duxbury Press.

Imai, M., & Haryu, E. (2001). Learning proper nouns and common nouns without clues from syntax. *Child Development,* **72,** 787–802.

Inhelder, B., & Piaget, J. (1969). *The early growth of logic in the child.* London: Routledge & Kegan Paul. (Original work published 1964)

Jaffe, J., Beebe, B., Feldstein, S., Crown, C., & Jasnow, M. (2001). Rhythms of dialogue in infancy. *Monographs of the Society for Research in Child Development,* **66** (2, Serial No. 265). Boston, MA: Blackwell.

Jusczyk, P. (1997). *The discovery of spoken language.* Cambridge, MA: MIT Press.

Jusczyk, P. (1999). How infants begin to extract words from speech. *Trends in Cognitive Science,* **3,** 323–328.

Just, M., & Carpenter, P. (1992). A capacity theory of comprehension: Individual differences in working memory. *Psychological Review,* **99,** 122–149.

Kagan, J. (1971). *Change and continuity in infancy.* New York: Wiley.

Kagan, J., Lapidus, D., & Moore, M. (1978). Infant antecedents of cognitive functioning. *Child Development,* **49,** 1005–1023.

Kahneman, D. (1973). *Attention and effort.* Englewood Cliffs, NJ: Prentice-Hall.

Klahr, D., and MacWhinney, B. (1998). Information processing. In W. Damon (Series Ed.) & D. Kuhn & R. Siegler (Vol. Eds.), *Handbook of child psychology: Vol. II. Cognition, perception, and language* (pp. 631–678). New York: Wiley.

Kuhn, T. (1962). *The structure of scientific revolutions.* Chicago: University of Chicago Press.

Kuhn, T. (1977). *The essential tension.* Chicago: University of Chicago Press.

Lifter, K. (1982). *Development of object related behavior during the transition from prelinguistic to linguistic communication.* Unpublished doctoral dissertation, Columbia University.

Lifter, K., & Bloom, L. (1989). Object play and the emergence of language. *Infant Behavior and Development,* **12**, 395–423.

Lifter, K., & Bloom, L. (1997). Intentionality and the role of play in the transition to language. In A. Wetherby, S. Warren, & J. Reichle (Eds.), *Transitions in prelinguistic communication* (Vol. 7, pp. 161–195). Baltimore, MD: Paul H. Brookes.

Lucariello, J. (1987). Concept formation and its relation to word learning and use in the second year. *Journal of Child Language,* **14**, 309–332.

Lucariello, J. (1995). Mind, culture, person: Elements in a cultural psychology. *Human Development,* **38**, 2–18.

Malatesta, C., Culver, C., Tesman, J., & Shepard, B. (1989). The development of emotion expression during the first two years of life. *Monographs of the Society for Research in Child Development,* **54** (Serial No. 219).

Malle, B., Moses, L., & Baldwin, D. (Eds.), (2001). *Intentions and intentionality: Foundations of social cognition.* Cambridge, MA: MIT Press.

Mandler, G. (1984). *Mind and body: Psychology of emotion and stress.* New York: Norton.

Margulis, M., & Anisfeld, M. (1991). *Two-year-olds reduce speech during effortful activities.* Poster presented at the biennial meeting of the Society for Research in Child Development, Seattle, WA.

Markman, E. (1989). *Categorization and naming in children.* Cambridge, MA: MIT Press.

Masur, E. (1982). Mothers' responses to infants' object-related gestures: Influences on lexical development. *Journal of Child Language,* **9**, 23–30.

McCall, R. (1972). Similarity in developmental profile among related pairs of human infants. *Science,* **178**, 1004–1005.

McCall, R., & McGhee, P. (1977). The discrepancy hypothesis of attention and affect in infants. In I. Uzgiris & F. Weizmann (Eds.) *The structure of experience* (pp. 179–210). New York: Plenum.

Nelson, K. (1974). Concept, word and sentence: Interrelations in acquisition and development, *Psychological Review,* **81**, 267–285.

Nelson, K. (1988). Constraints on word learning. *Cognitive Development,* **3**, 221–246.

Ninio, A., & Bruner, J. (1978). The achievement and antecedents of labeling. *Journal of Child Language,* **5**, 1–15.

Ninio, A., & Snow, C. (1996). *Pragmatic development.* Boulder, CO: Westview Press.

Oatley, K., & Johnson-Laird, P. (1987). Towards a cognitive theory of emotions. *Cognition and Emotion,* **1**, 29–50.

Overton, W. (1998). Developmental psychology: Philosophy, concepts, and methodology. In W. Damon (Series Ed.) & R. Lerner (Vol. Ed.), *Handbook of child psychology:* Vol. I. *Theoretical models of human development* (pp. 107–188). New York: Wiley.

Overton, W. (2002). Development across the life span: Philosophy, concepts, and theory. In I. Weiner (Editor-in-Chief) & R. Lerner, M. Easterbrooks, & J. Mistry (Eds.) *2002 Comprehensive handbook of psychology: Developmental psychology* (Vol. 6). New York: Wiley (in press).

Pashler, H. (1994). Dual-task interference in simple tasks: Data and theory. *Psychological Bulletin,* **116**, 220–244.

Phillips, R., & Sellito, V. (1990). Preliminary evidence on emotions expressed by children during solitary play. *Play and Culture,* **3**, 79–90.

Piaget, J. (1952). *The origins of intelligence in children.* New York: International Universities Press. (Originally published in 1936)

Piaget, J. (1954). *The construction of reality in the child.* New York: Basic Books. (Originally published in 1937)

Piaget, J. (1962). *Play, dreams and imitation in childhood.* New York: Norton (Originally published in 1952)

Piaget, J. (1967). *The child's conception of space.* New York: Norton. (Originally published in 1948)

Piaget, J. (1974). *Understanding causality.* New York: Norton. (Originally published in 1971)

Pinker, S. (1994). *The language instinct.* New York: Harper Collins.

Pinker, S. (1999). *Words and rules.* New York: Basic Books.

Renninger, A. (1990). Children's play interests, representation, and activity. In R. Fivush & J. Hudson (Eds.), *Emory Symposia in Cognition, Knowing and remembering in young children.* New York: Cambridge.

Renninger, A., & Wozniak, R. (1985). Effect of interest on attentional shift, recognition, and recall in young children. *Developmental Psychology, 21,* 624–632.

Ricciuti, H., & Poresky, R. (1972). Emotional behavior and development in the first year of life: An analysis of arousal, approach-withdrawal, and affective responses. In A. Pick (Ed.), *Minnesota symposia on child psychology* (Vol. 6, pp. 69–96). Minneapolis: University of Minnesota Press.

Rogoff, B. (1982). Integrating context and cognitive development. In M. Lamb & A. Brown (Eds.), *Advances in developmental psychology* (Vol. 2, pp. 125–170). Hillsdale, NJ: Erlbaum.

Rogoff, B. (1990). *Apprenticeship in thinking: Cognitive development in social context.* New York: Oxford University Press.

Rogoff, B. (1993). Children's guided participation and participatory appropriation in socio-cultural activity. In R. Wozniak & K. Fischer (Eds.), *Development in context: Acting and thinking in specific environments* (pp. 121–153). Hillsdale, NJ: Erlbaum.

Rovee-Collier (1997). Dissociations in infant memory: Rethinking the development of implicit and explicit memory. *Psychological Review, 104,* 467–498.

Ruff, H., & Lawson, K. (1990). Development of sustained focused attention in young children during free play. *Developmental Psychology, 26,* 85–93.

Rumelhart, D., & McClelland, J. (1986). On learning the past tense of English verbs. In J. McClelland, D. Rumelhart, & the PDP Research Group (Eds.), *Parallel distributed processing: Explorations in the microstructure of cognition: Vol. 2. Psychological and biological models* (pp. 216–271). Cambridge, MA: MIT

Schieffelin, B. (1983). Looking and talking: The functions of gaze direction in the conversations of a young child and her mother. In E. Ochs and B. Schieffelin (Eds.), *Acquiring conversational competence* (pp. 50–65). London: Routledge & Kegan Paul.

Searle, J. (1983). *Intentionality: An essay in the philosophy of mind.* Cambridge: Cambridge University Press.

Searle, J. (1992). *The rediscovery of the mind.* Cambridge, MA: MIT Press.

Sheets-Johnstone, M. (2000). Kinetic tactile-kinestheric bodies: Ontogenetical foundations of apprenticeship learning. *Human Studies, 23,* 343–370.

Shore, C. (1995). *Individual differences in language development.* Thousand Oaks, CA: Sage.

Skinner, B.F. (1957). *Verbal behavior.* New York: Appleton-Century-Crofts.

Smith, L. (2000). Learning how to learn words: An associative crane. In R. Golinkoff, K. Hirsh-Pasek, N. Akhtar, L. Bloom. G. Hollich, L. Smith, M. Tomasello, & A. Woodward, *Becoming a word learner: A debate on lexical acquisition* (pp. 51–80). New York: Oxford University Press.

Spelke, E. (1991). Physical knowledge in infancy: Reflections on Piaget's theory. In S. Carey & R. Gelman (Eds.), *The epigenesis of mind: Essays on biology and cognition* (pp. 133–169). Hillsdale, NJ: Erlbaum.

Sperber & Wilson (1986). *Relevance: Communication and cognition.* Cambridge, MA: Harvard University Press.

Sroufe, A., & Waters, E. (1976). The ontogenesis of smiling and laughter: A perspective on the organization of development in infancy. *Psychological Review, 83,* 173–189.

Stechler, G., & Carpenter, G. (1967). A viewpoint on early affective development. In J. Hellmuth (Ed.), *Exceptional infant: The normal infant* (Vol. 1, pp. 164–189). Seattle: Special Child Publications.

Stein, N., & Levine, L. (1987). Thinking about feelings: The development and origins of emotional knowledge. In R. Snow & M. Farr (Eds.), *Aptitude, learning, and instruction:* Vol. 3. *Cognition, conation, and affect* (pp. 165–197). Hillsdale, NJ: Erlbaum.

Stern, D. (1985). *The interpersonal world of the infant.* New York: Basic Books.

Sternberg, R., & Grigorenko, E. (2001). The (mis)organization of psychology. *APS Observer,* 14, 1ff.

Tamis-LeMonda, C. S., Bornstein, M. H., & Baumwell, L. (2001). Maternal responsiveness and children's achievement of language milestones. *Child Development, 72,* 748–767.

Taylor, C. (1979). Action as expression. In C. Diamond & J. Teichman (Eds.), *Intentions and intentionality, Essays in honor of G. E. M. Anscombe* (pp. 73–89). Ithaca, NY: Cornell University Press.

Taylor, C. (1985). *Philosophical papers: Vol. 1. Human agency and language.* Cambridge: Cambridge University Press.

Thelen, E. (2000). Grounded in the world: Developmental origins of the embodied mind. *Infancy,* 1, 3–28.

Thelen, E., & Smith, L. (1994). *A dynamic systems approach to the development of cognition and action.* Cambridge, MA: MIT Press.

Tomasello, M. (1988). The role of joint attentional processes in early language development. *Language Sciences,* 10, 69–88.

Tomasello, M. (1992). The social bases of language acquisition. *Social Development,* 1, 67–87.

Tomasello, M. (1995). Language is not an instinct. *Cognitive Development,* 10, 131–156.

Tomasello, M. (1999). *The cultural origins of human cognition.* Cambridge, MA: Harvard University Press.

Tomasello, M., & Akhtar, N. (1995). Two-year-olds use pragmatic cues to differentiate reference to objects and actions. *Cognitive Psychology,* 10, 201–224.

Tomasello, M., & Farrar, J. (1986). Joint attention and early language. *Child Development,* 57, 1454–1463.

Tomasello, M., & Kruger, A. (1992). Joint attention on actions: Acquiring verbs in ostensive and non-ostensive contexts. *Journal of Child Language,* 19, 311–333.

van Geert, P. (1991). A dynamic systems model of cognitive and language growth. *Psychological Review,* 98, 3–53.

Vygotsky, L. (1962). *Thought and language.* Cambridge MA: The MIT Press.

Vygotsky, L. (1978). *Mind in society, The development of higher psychological processes.* M. Cole, V. John-Steiner, S. Scribner, & E. Souberman (Eds.). Cambridge MA: Harvard University Press. (Originally published in 1930)

Werner, H., & Kaplan, B. (1963). *Symbol formation.* New York: Wiley

Wikstrom, P. (1994). *The role of attention in early cognitive development.* Unpublished doctoral dissertation, Teachers College, Columbia University.

Wohlwill, J. (1970). The age variable in psychological research. *Psychological Review,* 77, 49–64.

Woodward, A., & Markman, E. (1998). Early word learning. In W. Damon (Series Ed.) & D. Kuhn & R. Siegler (Vol. Eds.), *Handbook of child psychology: Vol. II. Cognition, perception, and language* (pp. 371–420). New York: Wiley.

Zelazo, P. (1972). Smiling and vocalizing: A cognitive emphasis. *Merrill-Palmer Quarterly,* 18, 349–365.

Zelazo, P. D., Astington, J., & Olson, D. (Eds.) (1999). *Developing theories of intention: Social understanding and self-control.* Mahwah, NJ: Erlbaum.

Zukow, P. (1990). Socio-perceptual bases for the emergence of language: An alternative to innatist approaches. *Developmental Psychobiology,* 23, 705–726.

ACKNOWLEDGMENTS

Richard Beckwith was a key player in virtually every aspect of the research we report in this *Monograph*, including but by no means limited to his intellectual contribution to the theoretical conceptualization behind the Intentionality Model and his empirical contribution to data collection and processing. He developed the original procedures for the lag sequential analysis and was a key member of the team that collected the video-recorded observations. Karin Lifter's dissertation research on the object play of three of the children (Lifter, 1982) provided the pilot data that led to the larger study of play (Lifter & Bloom, 1989), which in turn provided the coded data used for the research reported here. Karin was a major influence on the design of the research project and the procedures that were used in the laboratory playroom and home visits. Joanne Bitetti Capatides and Jeremie Hafitz were part of the original team that created the project and collected the longitudinal data. In addition, Joanne took the lead in developing the procedures for coding children's affect expression, and Jeri developed the original procedures for transcribing the children's speech. Rick Booth designed, and Abdur Raqib built, the video-computer interface used for collecting and processing the data. The procedures and formulas used in computing baselines for the lag sequential analysis were developed by Richard Beckwith with assistance from Erin Tinker and Adam Meyers and consultation with Robert Beckwith, Karen Clark, James Corter, and Jane Monroe. Pia Wikstrom verified the onset and offset times of the play episodes. Kathleen Bloom provided important statistical consultation that was invaluable for interpretation of the data. The research would not have been possible without the dedicated research assistants who helped in data collection, transcription, and coding, especially Virginia Brennan, Wei Chang, Roxanne DeMatteo, Suzanne Gottlieb, Margaret Honey, Cheryl Margulis, Adam Meyers, Marriette Newton-Danilo, Matthew Rispoli, Tresmaine Roubaine-Grimes, Scott Scheer, Jennifer Saldano, Anne Spangler, Lisa Spiegel, and Joy Vaughn-Brown.

Most important, however, we thank the children and their mothers for their interest, enthusiasm, and loyal participation in the research. They visited our laboratory playroom every month for almost two years (only one visit was missed by a single child), and they welcomed us with video-recorders into their homes for collecting auxiliary data. They let us become a part of their lives at a critical period in the children's development, and whatever contribution this research might make to understanding children's development is owed to them. Their contribution to this *Monograph* cannot be measured.

The research project was made possible by generous funding support from the Spencer Foundation, the National Science Foundation, and a Research Professorship and Dean's Grant from Teachers College, Columbia University. Please address correspondence and reprint requests to Lois Bloom, 95 Wilson Road, Easton, CT 06612 (*lmb32@columbia.edu*).

COMMENTARY

INTEGRATION: AN AGENDA FOR DEVELOPMENTAL RESEARCH

Ellin Kofsky Scholnick

This *Monograph* provides a solution to a problem bedeviling many developmentalists. Beset with the inadequacies of atomistic theories and artificial experimental tasks, they wonder how to create a different paradigm without losing credibility. The experimental method and its reductionist philosophical underpinnings have been the source both of psychology's greatest triumphs and of its deepest errors (Overton, 2002). What works well in physics and sensory psychology is deeply problematical for many areas of psychology. Attempts to reduce humans to their common denominator and to create a uniform context devoid of personal meaning led psychologists down many wrong pathways. The study of memory through paired associations of nonsense syllables created the impression of a pure function, when in fact memory is intimately involved with the knowledge base and affect. What one remembers and how much one remembers are tied to what one needs to know and what one knew before. Narrowing the scope of human reasoning to the ability to interpret the proposition *if p then q* made adults seem irrational and posed a paradox (Falmagne, 2000; Johnson-Laird & Byrne, 1991): Why are the investigators of reasoning so adept at induction and deduction when the educated adults they study are not? In actuality, preschoolers reason well in countering threats and evading rules. A reasoning problem misconstrued when couched in symbolic terms is flawlessly handled when couched as a permission statement (Cheng & Holyoak, 1985). Associationist and connectionist models divorce the learner from a rich context and simplify the internal products and processes of learning. The models omit many of the stratagems, such as analogy, that enable people to adapt with little effort to the exigencies of daily life.

92

In this *Monograph* and elsewhere Bloom (1998, 2000a, 2000b) has noted that developmental psychology is particularly disadvantaged. As theorists have decontextualized the child, they have compensated by positing a rich set of inbuilt processors or content constraints. Efforts to break apart the functions within the individual or the cues within the environment led to the creation of artificial tasks that bear a weak relationship to children's actual performance in their daily lives. A developmental picture is created of the universal child pursuing a solitary path through a barren landscape (Scholnick, 1999, 2000). The child's progress appeared to be astonishingly fast (Chomsky, 1988) or remarkably slow (Inhelder & Piaget, 1958).

Word learning, one focus of Bloom's research, is a case in point. The paradigmatic word learning scenario requires that the child learn a nonsense syllable to label an event or object without many contextual cues or any reason to learn it (e.g., Hirsh-Pasek, Golinkoff, & Hollich, 2000). If the event or object is complex, the reference is so indeterminate that the child may need to rely on strategies induced from other naming situations or inbuilt constraints to figure out the meaning of the word. Yet, typically, there is an environment rich in cues to meaning and a child in that environment who wants to learn the meaning in order to fulfill some purpose. Learning a word is not an isolated accomplishment, because the word refers to a constantly changing conceptual system (Bloom, 1993). Learning a gender term is not like discovering the name of some strange, useless object. Instead, the new word is an entry into a conceptual system that marks age (girl), marital status (Miss), place in a kinship system (daughter), occupation (actress), and even species (human). The child must learn the diverse children who can be called girls. Gender is marked syntactically (e.g., in pronouns) and socially. Girls and boys at different ages hear different samples of the gender language, and they may pick up different aspects of the gender system (Jacobson & Scholnick, 1999).

Bloom's critique has been voiced by many developmental psychologists (Falmagne, 2000; Lerner, 1998; Nelson, Henseler, & Plesa, 2000; Overton, 1998, 2002). Making the argument is easy. The daunting challenge is forging new paradigms and testable theories that overcome ingrained habits of atomistic analysis. Ultimately, some form of data reduction is necessary. How can one describe the dynamically changing, embodied child situated in an environment at a suitable level of generality? How can one describe integration and measure it? Bloom poses a theory and methodology to address the active, integrated, situated child. The agenda is ambitious, and this *Monograph* is just a sample of a larger theoretical and empirical program (e.g., Bloom, 1993, 1998, 2000a, 2000b). My comments focus on Bloom's answers to these questions and the further questions her answers raise.

The Active Child

A central task for developmentalists is explaining change. The external conditions that enable change and the products of change are observable, but the motivation for change is not. Consequently, the principles that describe how changes occur are usually hidden and they constitute the metatheoretical apparatus of theories of learning and development. Bloom's developmental principles are part of her metatheoretical apparatus. They serve two functions: as descriptors of developmental change (Bloom, 1993) much like Werner's (1948) orthogenetic principle, and as causes.

Relevance defines the focus of attention, the content matter of change. It is at the core of Bloom's belief in the intentional child, when intention takes the narrower meaning of purposive. The search for meaning is the prime motivational force for understanding human psychology in general and developmental psychology in particular. Models of development that divorce the children from their purposes and past experiences are artifices. The demands on a theory that brings relevance to its center are manifold. What defines relevance and how do you develop a theory of relevance—one that is personal and contextual—at a sufficiently general level? This is the obstacle theorists confront when they attempt to move from an atomistic, decontextualized theory to a situated one. Additionally, how precisely does relevance work to foster, hamper, integrate, or transform interpretation and expression? Bloom's discussion of and measurement of engagement may provide an entry into the scientific study of relevance.

Relevance defines the locus of change but not why and how it occurs. Many events capture attention, but relatively few produce change. The principles of discrepancy and elaboration are both definitions of development and the sources of change. Growth in symbolic capacity is encompassed in the principle of discrepancy, and changes in the knowledge base are captured by both principles.

Bloom has discussed discrepancy in two ways. Earlier, Bloom (1993) defined the term narrowly. During development, conceptual representations become increasingly distant from events in the immediate context (Werner & Kaplan, 1963). Word meanings, and the representations they signal, become anticipatory and abstract. The principle of discrepancy has solid empirical support in Sigel's (1993) examination of the impact of distancing and Nelson's (1996, 1999) analysis of the transformation of event representations into conceptual categories. In this *Monograph* and elsewhere (e.g., Bloom, 1993) it has been demonstrated that children increasingly use single words to refer to absent events and that their object play increasingly refers to imagined thematic relations. The empirical question is, "Does discrepancy play a causal role in developmental change?" Bloom has claimed that the increasing discrepancy between the contents of the child's mind and the immediate situation causes the child to look for means of expression that can convey the decontextualized content. Language becomes an instrument for doing so. Thus, the child begins to play and to use words more abstractly at about the same time as he or she enters the vocabulary spurt, which is often characterized as a time when the child knows the properties and functions of words.

In this *Monograph*, Bloom and Tinker adopt a broader definition of discrepancy. Faced with a mismatch between what they know and what they encounter, children seek ways to resolve the differences. This broader definition supplies Bloom's theory with more causal power and creates an even closer link between conceptual and linguistic advances. Problem solving to reduce discrepancies is a cognitive mechanism applicable to other domains, such as language. Although the principle of discrepancy resembles equilibration (Piaget, 1985), there are critical differences. Detecting a puzzle does not guarantee finding a solution. In Piaget's theory, the child often constructs the solution alone and the solutions are often generated from attempts to resolve inherent contradictions in the child's reasoning and concepts. Bloom and Tinker focus on the whole child integrated into a rich environment. They posit multiple, redundant cues in the social and physical environment to guide the discovery and use of knowledge, as well as diverse psychological functions that provide meaningful and accessible sources of solutions. The discrepancies the child must resolve result from gaps in knowledge and misconstrual of the situation and the messages sent by conversational partners. The intentionality model requires a road map to the difficulties children encounter and the advances that enable them to overcome these difficulties. An integrated model of development necessitates embedding each development, such as the transition from first words to multiword sentences, into a detailed interconnected developmental theory (see Bloom, 1993).

Elaboration is the most elusive developmental principle. Like discrepancy, elaboration is definitional to development. More mature individuals both differentiate aspects of events and form the links among elements. Like discrepancy, the principle serves as a reminder that the acquisition of a label is not the terminus of development because the referent becomes more abstract and interconnected. The novel theoretical claim is that elaboration is both the product of change and its source. The growth of one system (e.g., cognition) may produce elaboration in a second system because that second system is not sufficiently complex to handle the new insights. For example, children's growing comprehension of the nature of plans leads to refinement in emotional expression and syntax. These changes may then enable the individual to further refine and enrich the system that instigated the change. But what produced growth in the

95

original system? The elaboration of knowledge and the ramifications of elaboration depend heavily on the principle of discrepancy.

Bloom and her colleagues have mined their data set to examine the consequences of elaboration through mapping the interplay between cognitive, affective, and social interaction. The principle of elaboration rests on a detailed theory of cognitive and emotional growth and a detailed research program that simultaneously gauges several areas of growth to tap their interrelations. As a consequence, the picture of development that emerges may be more complicated than Bloom suggests. Integrating affect, language and cognition is difficult in a single act of communication, not merely because of the effort it takes. The material from one channel may conflict with another (Goldin-Meadow, 2002). Additionally, during the course of acquisition, it is often hard to find the right vehicle for mapping cognition onto emotional and linguistic output. A further agenda for the theory is a description of how elaborated states produce developmental change.

The Integrated Child

The principles of relevance, discrepancy, and elaboration set the parameters for macrodevelopmental changes during childhood. Integration occurs as the child finds coordinated outlets for expressing feelings and beliefs, and refines these outlets to convey more complex and abstract intentional states to conversational partners. Bloom's principles of change and integration are general and global. Coordination also occurs on the microlevel. Bloom adopts a model of online processing, derived from experimental psychology, that differs markedly from her descriptions of the principles of development. The fundamental units of analysis are various means of communicating intentional states vying for expression in a child with limited capacity and limited mastery over the expressive resources. Hence, trade-offs arise among systems. These trade-offs shift depending on the child's level of expressive competence and the tasks at hand. The model of competition for expressive resources rests on strong empirical grounds (see Case, 1992, and Pascual-Leone & Johnson, 1999, for examples in the developmental literature). The description of the dynamics of interacting systems provides the testable hypotheses that guide her empirical research and set an important agenda for future theoretical refinement. A model of an integrated child situated in an environment requires a full picture of the nature of the parameters of interaction.

Bloom posits two opposing internal principles that guide the interpretation or expression of language: engagement and effort. The test of the theory and its potential utility as a model of development rests on an examination of the patterns of operation of these two factors at different points of development. Engagement is a measurable outcome of relevance. Engagement taps attentional focus, social connectedness, and affective state. The child's low level of engagement may reflect lack of interest or scattered focus in an overly demanding environment, though attributing the sources of low engagement is difficult. Engagement is also nonlinear. Too little engagement prevents learning; too much involvement can be disruptive, narrowing focus or flooding the system. There is an optimal level of engagement, which Bloom calls *neutral affect*, when children can use their full expressive capacity. The factors that produce this optimal level and its expansions in capacity over time are yet to be determined.

Effort arises from the processing load on the individual. Most models of effort focus on the disruption of performance when multitasking creates excessive processing load. In this monograph and elsewhere, Bloom and Tinker are extraordinarily clever in pointing out the diverse ways processing demands disrupt performance and the integration of systems. Multiple comparisons tap the impact of effort, such as the output of skilled versus less skilled children and performance in demanding versus undemanding tasks. Usually, the level of expression is damped but there is less clarity in the pattern of damping. Like many investigators who examine the impact of processing load (e.g., Case, 1992; Fischer & Granott, 1995), Bloom needs to specify in advance the amount of effort required to disrupt performance and the nature of the disruption. Ideally, in each of the tests of the hypotheses the extent to which a particular system is damped or heightened and the pattern of expression should be the same. Yet, efforts to produce multiword speech are more disruptive than the production of first words and the temporal patterns of expression differ when the target is production of speech as opposed to toy play. Sometimes the child appears to suppress affect during word production and then releases expression, and at other times the recovery is much slower. Studies such as this may be hampered because there is no standard metric for units of effort.

Bloom has made a tremendous advance by placing language, emotion, and cognition into the context of a central, internal processing system. Having established that systems interact, Bloom is in a position to construct a developmental theory that can predict and explain these interactions. Further analysis of the data may yield very rich information about which system is traded off in the service of another. Such analyses are germane to a classic question about the relations between language and thought in task performance and in developmental change. This theoretical and research agenda is complicated because the nature of integration changes (Nelson, 1999; Scholnick, 2002). Thought becomes linguistic and language becomes more conceptual. Eventually, it is impossible to separate cognitive from linguistic demands because language and thought have been fused into a powerful symbolic system. Whereas in a moment-to-moment interchange the child may suppress one system to dwell on the other, often each system is brought to bear to support the other. In the course of development the systems transform one another. In a classic monograph, Flavell (1972) provided a taxonomy of developmental sequences that might be employed in ontogenesis and possibly microgenesis, too. Another agenda item is the further study of social interchange which is influenced by many pragmatic considerations as well as effort and engagement.

The Situated Child and the Observational Method

The effort-engagement model provides the quantitative predictive model to frame and test hypotheses about actions in context. Classic models of information processing are tested in experimental situations. Similarly, studies of the strategies that guide language acquisition are often tested through constrained tasks that do not lend themselves to a description of the situated, embodied child. Bloom's research group has taken four steps to translate the model of the situated child acting as a purposive information processing system into a scientifically rigorous paradigm.

1. They are among the few investigative teams to examine when the child *uses* language as a medium of expression and how the division of labor among expressive resources changes during development (see also Goldin-Meadow, 2002). They use conversation and object play the way cardiologists use stress tests—to tap how different avenues of expression are used during cognitively and socially demanding interchanges by children who vary in linguistic and emotional capacities. Their model provides the potential to switch focus and examine not merely how other systems are expressed when speech and play are the focus of activities, but also how speech and play are integrated when emotion is expressed.

2. Bloom studies children in a natural setting that affords a rich panoply of cues for the child to use in decoding language and expressing it. Experimental investigations of phenomena like word learning test whether a particular condition or combination of cues is sufficient for acquisition (e.g., Hirsh-Pasek et al., 2000). The experimental setting vests control in the experimenter. However, the child may perform differently when performance is purposive and when the child can choose the facets of environment that are relevant. In the observational setting, language, which is designed for communication, is studied through

the child's communications. The observational data present the opportunity for developing a taxonomy of use in which different expressive media are marshaled differently depending on the purposes of conversation and the input of the conversational partner. Moreover, conversational data can be used to study cognitive growth. It is the medium where children detect and resolve discrepancies and where they test out insights.

3. Using conversational data presents many pitfalls, not the least of which is data reduction. In experiments, the stimulus material and task environment constrain the data. In observational settings, the data may be collected under widely varying conditions and the constraints may be provided by a coding system that reflects the author's framework rather than the child's. The burden of the analysis falls on the use of reliable and valid coding systems. Bloom and her research team overlay their data collection with sophisticated measurements of affect and play productions, solidly grounded in the empirical literature. Children differ in their rates of expression, and different kinds of expression differ in the amount of time required. Here an ingenious method is used to determine the pattern of expression relative to the child's baseline of expression. The curves that depict the timing of expression become the source of the dependent variables and the focus of empirical analysis.

4. The analyses are accompanied by examination of individual differences often assessed by independent measures. Thus, Bloom is able to use parental assessment of vocabulary and earlier observed emotionality to chart online use of media of expression. The approach has the rich potential for both charting interactions and for other assessments of emotional, cognitive, and linguistic expressiveness. These data can provide sources of mutual validation and enhance the scientific rigor of the research. Consequently, Bloom and her colleagues can examine what the child is doing, what the child is expressing linguistically and emotionally, and what the child's conversational partners say and do. Thus, the act of speaking is put back into its emotional, social, and cognitive context.

Summary

In their magnum opus, Lakoff and Johnson (1999) argued for a philosophy in the flesh. The research presented in the *Monograph* describes psychology in the flesh. There are ways to measure the changing constellations of interacting systems that influence and transform one another

99

during development and many models to conceptualize the resulting patterns (Flavell, 1972). Development may consist of changing patterns of transactions among internal and external systems (Oyama, 1999). As Bloom and Tinker note, "Development leads to a variety of different abilities. . . . However, another developmental task not ordinarily considered is the integration of these abilities . . . in a seamless pattern of contingency in everyday events." Development consists of more than acquisition; it consists of changing patterns of integration, and changing patterns of use of multifaceted abilities.

References

Bloom, L. (1993). *The transition from infancy to language: Acquiring the power of expression.* New York: Cambridge University Press.

Bloom, L. (1998). Language acquisition in its developmental context. In D. Kuhn & R. S. Siegler (Eds.), *Handbook of child psychology*: Vol. 2. *Cognition, perception, and language* (pp. 309–370). New York: Wiley.

Bloom, L. (2000a). The intentionality model of word learning: How to learn a word, any word. In R. Golinkoff, K. Hirsh-Pasek, L. Bloom, L. Smith, A. Woodward, N. Akhtar, M. Tomasello, & G. Hollich, Becoming a word learner: A debate on lexical acquisition (pp. 19–50). New York, Oxford University Press.

Bloom, L. (2000b). Pushing the limits on theories of word learning. Commentary on G. Hollich, K. Hirsh-Pasek, & R. M. Golinkoff, Breaking the language barrier: An emergentist coalition model for the origins of word learning. *Monographs of the Society for Research in Child Development*, **65** (3, Serial No. 262, 124–135).

Case, R. (1992). *The mind's staircase.* Hillsdale, NJ: Erlbaum.

Cheng, P. W., & Holyoak, K. J. (1985). Pragmatic reasoning schemas. *Cognitive Psychology*, **17**, 391–416.

Chomsky, N. (1988). *Language and problems of knowledge.* Cambridge, MA: MIT Press.

Falmagne, R. J. (2000). Positionality and thought: On the gendered foundations of thought, culture, and development. In P. H. Miller & E. K. Scholnick (Eds.), *Toward a feminist developmental psychology* (pp. 191–213). New York: Routledge.

Fischer, K. W., & Granott, N. (1995). Beyond one-dimensional change: Parallel, concurrent, socially distributed processes in learning and development. *Human Development*, **38**, 302–314.

Flavell, J. H. (1972). An analysis of cognitive developmental sequences. *Genetic Psychology Monographs*, **86**, 279–350.

Goldin-Meadow, S. (2002). From thought to hand: Structured and unstructured communication outside of conventional language. In E. Amsel & J. Byrnes (Eds.), *Language, literacy, and cognitive development: The development and consequences of symbolic communication* (pp. 121–152). Mahwah, NJ: Erlbaum.

Hirsh-Pasek, K., Golinkoff, R. M., & Hollich, G. M. (2000). An emergentist coalition model for word learning: Mapping words to objects is the product of the interaction of multiple cues. In R. M. Golinkoff, K. Hirsh-Pasek, L. Bloom, L. B. Smith, A. L. Woodward, N. Akhtar, M. Tomasello, & G. Hollich, *Becoming a word learner: A debate on lexical acquisition* (pp. 136–164). New York: Oxford University Press

Inhelder, B., & Piaget, J. (1958). *The growth of logical thinking from childhood to adolescence.* New York: Basic Books.

Jacobson, J., & Scholnick, E. K (1999, April). *Learning about gender.* Poster session presented at the biennial meeting of the Society for Research in Child Development, Albuquerque, NM.

Johnson-Laird, P. N., & Byrne, R. M. (1991). *Deduction.* Hillsdale, NJ: Erlbaum.

Lakoff, G., & Johnson, M. (1999). *Philosophy in the flesh: The embodied mind and its challenge to Western thought.* New York: Basic Books.

Lerner, R. M. (1998). Theories of human development: Contemporary perspectives. In R. M. Lerner (Vol. Ed.), *Handbook of child psychology:* Vol. 1. *Theoretical models of human development* (pp. 1–24). New York: Wiley.

Nelson, K. (1996). *Language in cognitive development: Emergence of the mediated mind.* New York: Cambridge University Press.

Nelson, K. (1999). Levels and modes of representation: Issues for the theory of conceptual change and development. In E. K. Scholnick, K. Nelson, S. A. Gelman, & P. H. Miller (Eds.), *Conceptual development: Piaget's legacy* (pp. 269–291). Mahwah, NJ: Erlbaum.

Nelson K., Henseler, S., & Plesa, D. (2000). Entering a community of minds: "Theory of mind" from a feminist standpoint. In P. H. Miller & E. K. Scholnick (Eds.), *Toward a feminist developmental psychology* (pp. 61–84). New York: Routledge.

Overton, W. F. (1998). Developmental psychology. Philosophy, concepts, and methodology. In R. M. Lerner (Ed.), *Theoretical models of human development* (Vol. 1, pp. 107–188), in W. Damon (Series Ed.), *Handbook of child psychology.* New York: Wiley.

Overton, W. F. (2002). Understanding, explanation, and reductionism: Finding a cure for Cartesian anxiety. In T. Brown & L. Smith (Eds.), *Reductionism and the development of knowledge.* Mahwah, NJ: Erlbaum.

Oyama, S. (1999). Locating development: Locating developmental systems. In E. K. Scholnick, K. Nelson, S. A. Gelman, & P. H. Miller (Eds.), *Conceptual development: Piaget's legacy* (pp. 185–208). Mahwah, NJ: Lawrence Erlbaum.

Pascual-Leone, J., & Johnson, J. (1999). A dialectical constructivist view of representation: Role of mental attention, executives and symbols. In I. E. Sigel (Ed.), *Theoretical perspectives in the development of representational (symbolic) thought* (pp. 169—200). Mahwah, NJ: Erlbaum.

Piaget, J. (1985). *The equilibration of cognitive structures.* Chicago: University of Chicago Press.

Scholnick, E. K. (1999). Representing logic. In I. E. Sigel (Ed.), *Theoretical perspectives in the development of representational(symbolic) thought* (pp. 113–128). Mahwah, NJ: Erlbaum.

Scholnick, E. K. (2000). Engendering development. Metaphors of change. In P. H. Miller & E. K. Scholnick (Eds.), *Toward a feminist developmental psychology* (pp. 61–83). New York: Routledge.

Scholnick, E. K. (2002). Language, literacy, and thought: Forming a partnership. In E. Amsel & J. Byrnes (Eds.), *Language, literacy, and cognitive development: The development and consequences of symbolic communication* (pp. 3–26). Mahwah, NJ: Erlbaum.

Sigel, I. E. (1993). The centrality of a distancing model for the development of representational competence. In R. R. Cocking & K. A. Renninger (Eds), *The development and meaning of psychological distance* (pp. 141–158). Hillsdale, NJ: Erlbaum.

Werner, H. (1948). *Comparative psychology of mental development.* Chicago: Follett.

Werner, H., & Kaplan, B. (1963). *Symbol formation.* New York: Wiley.

Lois Bloom (Ph.D., Columbia University, 1968) is Edward Lee Thorndike Professor Emeritus of Psychology and Education at Teachers College, Columbia University. Her research interests have centered on early language acquisition, in general, and the part played by developments in emotion and cognition, in particular, on language development.

Erin Tinker (M.A., New York University, 1990; M.A., Teachers College, Columbia University, 1993) is Learning Specialist at The Trinity School in New York City.

Ellin Kofsky Scholnick (Ph.D., University of Rochester, 1963) is Professor of Psychology and Associate Provost for Faculty Affairs at the University of Maryland, College Park. She is coeditor of *The Developmental Psychology of Planning: Why, How, and When Do We Plan?*; *Blueprints for Thinking: The Role of Planning in Cognitive Development*; *New Trends in Conceptual Development: Challenges to Piaget's Theory?*; *Conceptual Development: Piaget's Legacy*; and *Toward a Feminist Developmental Psychology*.

STATEMENT OF EDITORIAL POLICY

The *Monographs* series is devoted to publishing developmental research that generates authoritative new findings and uses these to foster fresh, better integrated, or more coherent perspectives on major developmental issues, problems, and controversies. The significance of the work in extending developmental theory and contributing definitive empirical information in support of a major conceptual advance is the most critical editorial consideration. Along with advancing knowledge on specialized topics, the series aims to enhance cross-fertilization among developmental disciplines and developmental subfields. Therefore, clarity of the links between the specific issues under study and questions relating to general developmental processes is important. These links, as well as the manuscript as a whole, must be as clear to the general reader as to the specialist. The selection of manuscripts for editorial consideration, and the shaping of manuscripts through reviews-and-revisions, are processes dedicated to actualizing these ideals as closely as possible.

Typically *Monographs* entail programmatic large-scale investigations; sets of programmatic interlocking studies; or—in some cases—smaller studies with highly definitive and theoretically significant empirical findings. Multi-authored sets of studies that center on the same underlying question can also be appropriate; a critical requirement here is that all studies address common issues, and that the contribution arising from the set as a whole be unique, substantial, and well integrated. The needs of integration preclude having individual chapters identified by individual authors. In general, irrespective of how it may be framed, any work that is judged to significantly extend developmental thinking will be taken under editorial consideration.

To be considered, submissions should meet the editorial goals of *Monographs* and should be no briefer than a minimum of 80 pages (including references and tables); the upper limit of 150–175 pages is more flexible (please submit four copies). Because a *Monograph* is inevitably lengthy and usually substantively complex, it is particularly important that the text be well organized and written in clear, precise, and literate English. Note, however, that authors from non-English-speaking countries should not be put off by this stricture. In accordance with the general aims of SRCD, this series is actively interested in promoting international exchange of developmental research. Neither membership in the Society nor affiliation with the academic discipline of psychology is relevant in considering a *Monographs* submission.

The corresponding author for any manuscript must, in the submission letter, warrant that all coauthors are in agreement with the content of the manuscript. The corresponding author also is responsible for informing all coauthors, in a timely manner, of manuscript submission, editorial decisions, reviews received, and any revisions recommended. Before publication, the corresponding author also must warrant in the submission letter that the study has been conducted according to the ethical guidelines of the Society for Research in Child Development.

Potential authors who may be unsure whether the manuscript they are planning would make an appropriate submission are invited to draft an outline of what they propose, and send it to the Editor for assessment. This mechanism, as well as a more detailed description of all editorial policies, evaluation processes, and format requirements, can be found at the Editorial Office web site (http://astro.temple.cdu/~overton/monosrcd.html) or by contacting the Editor, Willis F. Overton, Temple University–Psychology, 1701 North 13th St.—Rm. 567, Philadelphia, PA 19122-6085 (e-mail: monosrcd@blue.vm.temple.edu) (telephone: 1-215-204-7718).

Monographs of the Society for Research in Child Development (ISSN 0037-976X), one of three publications of the Society for Research in Child Development, is published four times a year by Blackwell Publishers, Inc., with offices at 350 Main Street, Malden, MA 02148, USA, and 108 Cowley Road, Oxford OX4 1JF, UK. Call US 1-800-835-6770, fax: (781) 388-8232, or e-mail: subscrip@ blackwellpub.com. A subscription to *Monographs of the SRCD* comes with a subscription to *Child Development* (published six times a year in February, April, June, August, October, and December). A combined package rate is also available with the third SRCD publication, *Child Development Abstracts and Bibliography*, published three times a year.

INFORMATION FOR SUBSCRIBERS   For new orders, renewals, sample copy requests, claims, change of address, and all other subscription correspondence, please contact the Journals Subscription Department at the publisher's Malden office.

INSTITUTIONAL SUBSCRIPTION RATES FOR MONOGRAPHS OF THE SRCD/CHILD DEVELOPMENT 2001   The Americas $293, Rest of World £192. All orders must be paid by credit card, business check, or money order. Checks and money orders should be made payable to Blackwell Publishers. Canadian residents please add 7% GST.

INSTITUTIONAL SUBSCRIPTION RATES FOR MONOGRAPHS OF THE SRCD/CHILD DEVELOPMENT/CHILD DEVELOPMENT ABSTRACTS AND BIBLIOGRAPHY 2001   The Americas $369, Rest of World £246. All orders must be paid by credit card, business check, or money order. Checks and money orders should be made payable to Blackwell Publishers. Canadian residents please add 7% GST.

BACK ISSUES   Back issues are available from the publisher's Malden office.

MICROFORM   The journal is available on microfilm. For microfilm service, address inquiries to Bell and Howell Information and Learning, 300 North Zeeb Road, Ann Arbor, MI 48106-1346, USA. Bell and Howell Serials Customer Service Department: 1-800-521-0600 ×2873.

POSTMASTER   Periodicals class postage paid at Boston, MA, and additional offices. Send address changes to Blackwell Publishers, 350 Main Street, Malden, MA 02148, USA.

CURRENT

United States Postal Service Statement of Ownership, Management, and Circulation (required by 39 U.S. C. 3685)(1) Publication Title: Child Development; (2) Publication No:889-020; (3) Filing Date: 9/15/01(4) Issue Frequency: six times in January/February, March/April, May/June, July/August, September/October, November/December(5) No. of issues published annually: 6; (6) Annual subscription price: $35.00 individual, $331.00 institutional; (7) Complete mailing address of known office of publication: Blackwell Publishers, 350 Main Street, Malden, MA 02148; (8) Complete mailing address of headquarters or general business office: Blackwell Publishers, 350 Main Street, Malden, MA 02148;(9) Full names and complete mailing addresses of publisher, editor, and managing editor, Blackwell Publishers, 350 Main Street, Malden, MA 02148; Editor, Marc Bornstein, National institute of Child Health and Human Development, 6705 Rockledge Dr, Ste 8030, Bethesda, MD 20892; Managing Editor, Jay Aiken, Society for Research in Child Development, University of Michigan, 505 East Huron, Ste 301, Ann Arbor, MI 48104(10) Owner, Society for Research in Child Development, University of Michigan, 505 E. Huron, Suite 301, Ann Arbor, MI 48104(11) Known bondholders, mortgagees, and other security holders owning or holding 1 percent or more of the total amount of bonds, mortgages, or other securities: None; (12) The purpose, function, and nonprofit status of this organization and the exempt status for federal income tax purposes: N/A; (13) Publication name:Child Development; (14) Issue date for circulation data below:72:4 July 2001; (15) Extent and nature of circulation: (a) Total no. copies (net press run); Average no. copies each issue during proceeding 12 months:9746; Actual no. copies of single issue published nearest to filing date:10248; (b) paid and/or requested circulation; (1) Paid/Requested Outside-County Mail Subscriptions Stated on Form 3541. (Include advertiser's proof and exchange copies) Average no. copies each issue during proceeding 12 months:8272; Actual no. copies of single issue published nearest to filing date:8743; (2) Paid In-County Subscriptions Stated on Form 3541 (Include advertiser's proof and exchange copies); Average no. copies each issue during proceeding 12 months: 0; Actual no. copies of single issue published nearest to filing date: 0; (2) Sales Through Dealers and Carriers, Street Vendors, Counter Sales, and Other Non USPS Paid Distribution; Average no. copies each issue during proceeding 12 months: 0; Actual no. copies of single issue published nearest to filing date: 0; (4) Other Classes Mailed Through USPS; Average no. copies each issue during proceeding 12 months: 0; Actual no. copies of single issue published nearest to filing date: 0; (c) Total paid and/or requested circulation (sum of 15b (1), (2), (3) and (4)) Average no. copies each issue during proceeding12 months:8272; Actual no. copies of single issue published nearest to filing date:8743; (d) Free distribution by mail (samples, complimentary, and other free) (1) Outside-County as Stated on Form 3541; Average no. copies each issue during proceeding 12 months:68; Actual no. copies of single issue published nearest to filing date: 0; (2) In-County as Stated on Form 3541; Average no. copies each issue during proceeding 12 months: 0; Actual no. copies of single issue published nearest to filing date: 0; (3) Other Classes Mailed Through the USPS; Average no. copies each issue during proceeding 12 months: 0; Actual no. copies of single issue published nearest to filing date:17; (f) Total free distribution (sum of 15d and 15e); Average no. copies each issue during proceeding 12 months:93; Actual no. copies of single issue published nearest to filing date:85; (g) Total distribution (sum of 15c and 15f); Average no. copies each issue during proceeding12 months:8365; Actual no. copies of single issue published nearest to filing date:8828; (h) copies not distributed; Average no. copies each issue during proceeding 12 months:1381; Actual no. copies of single issue published nearest to filing date:1420; (i) Total (sum of 15g and h); Average no. copies each issue during proceeding12 months: 9746; Actual no. copies of single issue published nearest to filing date:10248; (j) Percent paid and/or requested circulation (15c/15gX100) Average no. copies each issue during proceeding12 months:99%Actual no. copies of single issue published nearest to filing date: 99%;(16) This Statement of Ownership will be printed in the November/December 2001 issue of this publication. (17) Signature and Title of Editor, Publisher, Business Manager or Owner: Barbara Sasso, Customer Service Manager, 9/15/01.I certify that all information furnished on this form is true and complete. I understand that anyone who furnishes false or misleading information on this form or who omits material or information requested on the form may be subject to criminal sanctions (including fines and imprisonment) and/or civil sanctions (including multiple damages and civil penalties).Failure to file or publish a statement of ownership may lead to suspension of second-class. authorization. PS Form 3526 October 1999 (Facsimile)